Penguin Monarchs

THE HOUSES OF WESSEX AND DENMARK

Athelstan	Tom Holland
Aethelred the Unready	Richard Abels
Cnut	Ryan Lavelle
Edward the Confessor	James Campbell

THE HOUSES OF NORMANDY, BLOIS AND ANJOU

William I	Marc Morris
William II	John Gillingham
Henry I	Edmund King
Stephen	Carl Watkins
Henry II	Richard Barber
Richard I	Thomas Asbridge
John	Nicholas Vincent

THE HOUSE OF PLANTAGENET

Henry III	Stephen Church
Edward I	Andy King
Edward II	Christopher Given-Wilson
Edward III	Jonathan Sumption
Richard II	Laura Ashe

THE HOUSES OF LANCASTER AND YORK

Henry IV	Catherine Nall
Henry V	Anne Curry
Henry VI	James Ross
Edward IV	A. J. Pollard
Edward V	Thomas Penn
Richard III	Rosemary Horrox

THE HOUSE OF TUDOR

Henry VII	Sean Cunningham
Henry VIII	John Guy
Edward VI	Stephen Alford
Mary I	John Edwards
Elizabeth I	Helen Castor

THE HOUSE OF STUART

James I	Thomas Cogswell
Charles I	Mark Kishlansky
[Cromwell	David Horspool]
Charles II	Clare Jackson
James II	David Womersley
William III & Mary II	Jonathan Keates
Anne	Richard Hewlings

THE HOUSE OF HANOVER

George I	Tim Blanning
George II	Norman Davies
George III	Amanda Foreman
George IV	Stella Tillyard
William IV	Roger Knight
Victoria	Jane Ridley

THE HOUSES OF SAXE-COBURG & GOTHA AND WINDSOR

Edward VII	Richard Davenport-Hines
George V	David Cannadine
Edward VIII	Piers Brendon
George VI	Philip Ziegler
Elizabeth II	Douglas Hurd

JOHN GUY

Henry VIII

The Quest for Fame

ALLEN LANE
an imprint of
PENGUIN BOOKS

ALLEN LANE

Published by the Penguin Group
Penguin Books Ltd, 80 Strand, London WC2R ORL, England
Penguin Group (USA) Inc., 375 Hudson Street, New York, New York 10014, USA
Penguin Group (Canada), 90 Eglinton Avenue East, Suite 700, Toronto, Ontario,
Canada M4P 2Y3 (a division of Pearson Penguin Canada Inc.)
Penguin Ireland, 25 St Stephen's Green, Dublin 2, Ireland (a division of Penguin Books Ltd)
Penguin Group (Australia), 707 Collins Street, Melbourne, Victoria 3008, Australia
(a division of Pearson Australia Group Pty Ltd)
Penguin Books India Pvt Ltd, 11 Community Centre, Panchsheel Park,
New Delhi – 110 017, India
Penguin Group (NZ), 67 Apollo Drive, Rosedale, Auckland 0632, New Zealand
(a division of Pearson New Zealand Ltd)
Penguin Books (South Africa) (Pty) Ltd, Block D, Rosebank Office Park, 181 Jan Smuts
Avenue, Parktown North, Gauteng 2193, South Africa

Penguin Books Ltd, Registered Offices: 80 Strand, London WC2R ORL, England

www.penguin.com

First published 2014
001

Copyright © John Guy, 2014

The moral right of the author has been asserted

Set in 9.5/13.5 pt Sabon LT Std
Typeset by Jouve (UK), Milton Keynes
Printed in Great Britain by Clays Ltd, St Ives plc

ISBN: 978-0-141-97712-6

www.greenpenguin.co.uk

MIX
Paper from
responsible sources
FSC   FSC® C018179
www.fsc.org

Penguin Books is committed to a sustainable
future for our business, our readers and our planet.
This book is made from Forest Stewardship
Council™ certified paper.

Contents

HENRY VIII

Introduction

Few monarchs have divided opinion more than Henry VIII. Inevitably so, because besides doing more than any other English king to reshape the country's institutions and identity in roughly the form they survive today, he was also a wilful destroyer. For those who opposed his attacks on the Church and hefty demands of taxation, he was a vindictive tyrant who associated might with right and value with lustre. He was, said John Hale, a priest of Isleworth in Middlesex, 'to be called a great tyrant rather than a king'. Allowed his day in court by Henry before being sent to the gallows on a charge of high treason, Hale was determined to put his views on the record. 'Since the realm of England was first a realm,' he insisted, 'was there never in it so great a robber and pillager of the commonwealth read of nor heard of as is our king.'[1]

Others have strenuously disagreed. For perhaps a majority of his subjects, Henry was everything a king should be. Capable of the best as well as the worst, he exuded magnificence, both personally and through his spectacular palaces and art collections. His children revered and adored him. Faced with disobedience from her own privy councillors, his daughter Mary, who as the country's first queen regnant sometimes found it an uphill struggle to establish her authority even with her closest supporters, declared that 'they would never have dared to do such a thing in her father's lifetime, and she only wished he might come to life again for a month'.[2]

Not surprisingly, criticisms of Henry's policies were linked to attacks on his private life. Comparing him to the infamous classical tyrant King Dionysius of Syracuse, Sir Thomas Elyot wrote:

> He was a man of quick and subtle wit, but therewith he was wonderful sensual, unstable and wandering in sundry affections. Delighting sometime in voluptuous pleasures, another time in gathering of great treasure and riches, oftentimes resolved into a beastly rage and vengeable cruelty. About the public weal of his country always remiss, in his own desires studious and diligent.[3]

But while Henry had six wives and several mistresses, he was, by the standards of his royal contemporaries, sexually restrained. And although two of his wives were executed and two divorced, it can be argued that dynastic security made such casualties necessary. Whereas those on the wrong side of Henry saw him as a tyrant ruled by his sexual passions, others (especially nobles and property owners keen to profit from the spoils of the annihilation of the abbeys) saw him as providing the essential stability that kept the country free of the civil wars that had plagued the fifteenth century or the wars of religion that would bring anarchy to France and the Netherlands later in the century.

Rather than attempt to vindicate the views of either side

of the debate in this short reassessment, I will seek to look behind the mask into Henry's mind and explain how he himself understood events. How far did those of his childhood and adolescence make their indelible mark? What led him to shape his policies and choose his wives and ministers? Was he a ruler with genuine principles or deeply held convictions or simply an unscrupulous pragmatist? Was he devout and therefore sincere in demanding the massive changes and destruction wreaked upon the Church and the monasteries? What impelled him to attempt to become a commanding presence on the European stage, with all its immense costs, human and material? In particular, did his cruel streak come only latterly with age, disappointment and ill-health, or was it always there?

Keeping such questions to the fore will, I hope, open the door to unfamiliar as well as more familiar insights and enable readers to feel they can reach out and touch this charismatic and yet so difficult and complex king.

Author's Note

Dates are given in the Old Style Julian calendar, but the year is assumed to have begun on 1 January, and not on Lady Day, the feast of the Annunciation (i.e. 25 March), which was by custom the first day of the calendar year in France, Spain and Italy until 1582, in Scotland until 1600, and in England, Wales and Ireland until 1752.

Spelling and orthography of primary sources in quotations are given in modernized form. Modern punctuation and capitalization are provided where there is none in the original manuscript.

Money appears in the pre-decimal form in use until 1971. There are twelve pence in a shilling (modern 5p or US 8 cents), twenty shillings in a pound (£1 or US$ 1.60), and so on. Modern equivalents for sixteenth-century figures are extremely difficult to calculate, as the effects of inflation and huge fluctuations in the relative values of land and commodities render modern equivalents misleading, but rough estimates may be obtained by multiplying all the numbers by a thousand.

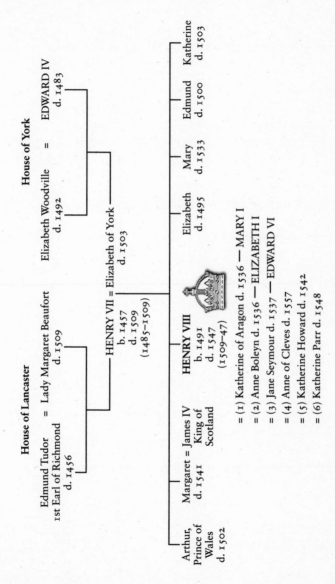

House of Lancaster

House of York

Edmund Tudor = Lady Margaret Beaufort
1st Earl of Richmond   d. 1509
d. 1456

Elizabeth Woodville = EDWARD IV
d. 1492   d. 1483

—— HENRY VII = Elizabeth of York ——
b. 1457   d. 1503
d. 1509
(1485–1509)

Arthur,
Prince of
Wales
d. 1502

Margaret = James IV
d. 1541   King of
Scotland

HENRY VIII
b. 1491
d. 1547
(1509–47)

Elizabeth
d. 1495

Mary
d. 1533

Edmund
d. 1500

Katherine
d. 1503

= (1) Katherine of Aragon d. 1536 — MARY I
= (2) Anne Boleyn d. 1536 — ELIZABETH I
= (3) Jane Seymour d. 1537 — EDWARD VI
= (4) Anne of Cleves d. 1557
= (5) Katherine Howard d. 1542
= (6) Katherine Parr d. 1548

Henry VIII

I
Shaping a Life

The boy who one day would become England's wealthiest and most powerful king was born on Tuesday 28 June 1491 at Greenwich. His birthplace, then, was little more than a Thamesside manor house, but one that, when demolished and rebuilt with suitably regal apartments and recreational facilities such as a tiltyard and a library, he would in later life make his second most visited palace.

The baby's father was the tall, supple, indefatigable King Henry VII. As the twenty-eight-year-old Earl of Richmond, this most improbable of rulers had captured the crown from the usurper Richard III, defeating him at the Battle of Bosworth in 1485 with the help of a contingent of Swiss-trained pikemen. Seeking to conjure up the feel of legitimacy, the victorious Henry VII had then married Elizabeth of York, the eldest daughter of Edward IV, the last rightful Yorkist king of England. Unusually for a royal mother, Elizabeth would become an important influence on young Henry's life as well as being the person who drew up the plans for the redesign of Greenwich Palace.

Named after his father, Henry was his parents' second son. His brother Arthur was five years older – and the age gap was significant. By the time Henry was weaned and learning to walk, their father had already invested Arthur as Prince of Wales and sent him to live at his princely capital at Ludlow in Shropshire, which meant that the two boys never really knew each other.

As a second son, Henry would be treated very differently. Until the age of eleven, he was kept 'among the women' in the nursery at Eltham, a smaller royal palace surrounded by a moat and in an idyllic setting, less than an hour's ride from Greenwich. In charge was Elizabeth Denton, one of his mother's most trusted servants, who also brought up Henry's sisters Margaret and Mary. Two other siblings, Elizabeth and Edmund, died young.

Henry adored his mother and always remembered Denton with affection, which suggests a largely happy childhood.[1] How secure he felt is something else, for his father was considered by many disgruntled Yorkists to be a usurper himself. While Henry was in the nursery, a dangerous conspiracy put forward the twenty-year-old pretender Perkin Warbeck as a potential king. Warbeck's backers included Margaret of York, the Dowager Duchess of Burgundy, Edward IV's youngest sister and a force to be reckoned with. She maintained that Warbeck was her long-lost nephew, Richard, Duke of York, otherwise said (according to the most plausible accounts) to have been murdered with his elder brother, Edward, in the Tower of London in 1483, after they were seized by their uncle, Richard III.

In an effort to discredit this imposter, Henry VII knighted his second son and created him Duke of York at the tender age of three, before parading him through the streets of

London, 'sitting alone upon a warhorse', to prove that he, and not Warbeck, was the real duke.[2] To stay upright in the saddle was a considerable feat for a boy so young. Prince Henry, who by his early twenties could exhaust up to ten horses a day while out hunting, must already have been a reasonably proficient horseman.

By 1495, Yorkist conspiracy was found to have penetrated deep into Henry VII's inner circle. It took him nearly three more years and a full-scale battle to defeat Warbeck; at the worst of the crisis, in June 1497, Elizabeth of York had to snatch her son, who would be six in a fortnight, in terror from his nursery and rush with him to the safety of the innermost ward of the Tower of London, where they stayed for a week, encircled by guards.

Henry's education began early, when his mother taught him to read and write. A recently discovered inscription, 'Thys Boke Is Myne, Prynce Henry', in his own inimitable hand, scrawled into his schoolboy copy of Cicero when he was eleven or twelve, adopts letter forms that closely resemble hers, as do many more of his numerous annotations in the same volume.[3]

Henry's first schoolmaster was the orator-poet John Skelton, who was appointed when his pupil was five or more likely six. 'The honour of England I learned to spell / In dignity royal that doth excel,' Skelton later boasted.[4] And, to make studying more congenial for her young son when he was eight, his mother – for almost certainly it was she – found him a mentor, barely out of his teens, to join him in the schoolroom. This was William Blount, Lord Mountjoy, stepson of her very own Lord Chamberlain. In 1499,

Mountjoy then arranged for his own tutor, Desiderius Erasmus of Rotterdam, the most stellar intellectual north of the Alps, to visit the nursery at Eltham, accompanied by his friend Thomas More. On their arrival, the royal children greeted the pair in the great hall of the palace while their attendants looked on. Prince Henry, who (said Erasmus) 'had already something of royalty in his demeanour, in which there was a certain dignity combined with a singular courtesy', was flanked by his two sisters, while their brother Edmund was a babe in arms.

At the close of the encounter, More presented Henry with a set of Latin verses, but had failed to warn Erasmus to do the same. At dinner afterwards, therefore, the Dutch scholar received 'a little note' from Henry pointedly highlighting what he clearly took to be a snub. Labouring red-faced late into the night for three days in his embarrassment, Erasmus composed a Latin ode of 150 lines, which he bundled up with some older verses scraped together from the bottom of his trunk and prefaced with a dedication advising Henry that only by being a patron of literature and the arts could he win immortal fame like that enjoyed by Alexander the Great. The verses still survive and are unremarkable, but the dedication is striking, since it suggests that Erasmus – himself no shrinking violet – had foreseen that the quest for fame and recognition would be what would chiefly motivate Henry as an adult. What the Dutchman had not bargained for was that Henry – who would indeed come to see Alexander's heroic example as one he wished to rival or even excel – would eventually imitate the worst as well as the best of Alexander's characteristics. For Alexander was famous not simply on account of his extraordinary bravery and his exceptional qualities, such as his generosity and patronage of the arts. He was also notorious for his territorial aggression, his ferocious desire for revenge when thwarted and his ambition to become immortal, to the extent that he even sometimes donned 'priestly' garments or dressed up as a god.[5]

Henry's earliest official act was performed at Windsor when, at the age of five, he witnessed a charter granting the monks of Glastonbury Abbey the right to hold two annual fairs.[6] Five years later, he undertook important duties at his elder brother's wedding. Since 1488, their father had been negotiating with the co-rulers of Spain, King Ferdinand of Aragon and his wife, Isabella of Castile, seeking a dynastic alliance by marrying Arthur to their youngest daughter, Katherine. The couple were betrothed by proxy in 1497, and Ferdinand and Isabella promised to send their daughter to England by the time that Arthur was fourteen.

When she finally arrived, Arthur was fifteen and his bride almost a year older. Among those greeting her at Southwark was the ten-year-old Prince Henry, who rode beside her through the London streets to the delight of the cheering crowds. The wedding was at Old St Paul's, where the young Henry escorted Katherine of Aragon into the nave of the church and then back after the nuptial Mass to the Bishop of London's palace for the marriage feast. The celebrations lasted for almost a fortnight, and Henry joined in enthusiastically. While dancing with his sister Margaret after a masque, he astonished everyone by ripping off his jacket and cavorting wildly in front of the guests.[7] Always the extrovert, he already knew how to steal the show at other people's parties.

After ascertaining whether Katherine was considered old enough by her parents to have regular sex, since Ferdinand and Isabella believed that they had lost their teenage son, Prince Juan, to a 'surfeit' of sex just a few years before, Henry VII sent Arthur and his bride back to Ludlow to live as man and wife. This was the zenith of his reign, when it looked as if he had everything under his control. The only serious setback had arisen shortly before Katherine first arrived in England. To the king's fury, one of the queen's closest living relatives, Edmund de la Pole, Earl of Suffolk, fearing arrest as a credible Yorkist claimant to the throne, had fled to Aachen with his brother Richard to seek the protection of the Holy Roman Emperor, Maximilian I.

Prince Henry's prospects, meanwhile, were dramatically transformed. On 2 April 1502, Arthur died at Ludlow.[8] What killed him is unknown. Commonly canvassed causes are bubonic plague, tuberculosis and testicular cancer.[9] But to the younger Henry, the diagnosis scarcely mattered, for now he, and not his older brother, would be the future king.

Elizabeth of York consoled her husband with the thought that they still had one 'fair, goodly and a towardly young prince' and were themselves still young enough to try for another.[10] Soon she was pregnant again, and on 2 February 1503, the feast of Candlemas, was successfully delivered of a daughter in the middle of the night.

Then, lightning struck twice. Elizabeth's accouchement had come upon her suddenly and her delivery was cruel.

She died shortly afterwards on the morning of her thirty-seventh birthday. Her baby, christened Katherine, also died.

For Henry, his mother's death was like a thunderbolt. Nothing had shaken him more, he wrote some years later, than first hearing the news that never would he see her again. Just an incidental, casual reference to his bereavement, he explained, could 'reopen a wound that time had begun to heal'.[11] A stranger to his elder brother, he had not been able to find grief in his heart for him, but for his mother he mourned intently. Her death was his first deep emotional experience, and he took it badly. Later in life, his sense of loss would return in the form of a desire for closeness with her side of the family, and it was on account of her that when he became king he would restore to favour many of her relations who had fallen under a cloud during his father's reign.

The major change in Henry's routine around this time was that Skelton was sent away and a team of new, heavyweight schoolmasters brought in. Led by John Holt, an innovative Latin tutor who knew both Erasmus and Thomas More and may have been recommended by one of them, the new team taught Henry to the highest standards in the liberal arts. He grew up to appreciate culture and the arts: he spoke French fluently and especially enjoyed studying music – he was soon proficient in playing the lute, recorder and keyboard instruments. Later he would compose his own songs as well as perform them. Nor would physical exercise be neglected: Henry, who always fancied himself as a sportsman, was particularly keen as an adolescent on archery and tennis.[12]

After Holt's death, William Hone, a graduate of the same Oxford college, headed the team. And the effects could be seen when, aged fifteen, Henry wrote a letter to Erasmus so flawless in its Latin style that the great scholar refused to believe it was the prince's own work. Only when Henry's schoolroom mentor, Mountjoy, showed him other examples of the prince's letters revealing the stages of composition was the great man persuaded.[13]

While Henry's new tutors kept him busy, an air of continual crisis pervaded his environment. After his wife's death, the worst side of Henry VII's character came to the fore. As Francis Bacon noted a century later, he became 'a dark prince and infinitely suspicious'.[14] And by striving to be feared rather than loved, Henry VII created a twilight world most dangerous for its unpredictability. From now on, he would be over-protective of his only surviving son. So when, in February 1504, the younger Henry was invested as Prince of Wales, he was not sent to Ludlow. Instead, his father meant to train him in the art of kingship himself.

Shortly after he was thirteen, therefore, Henry was recalled from Eltham to Greenwich to live at Court, where his father could watch over him. And from then onwards the prince shadowed his father, saying little. When later the Spanish ambassador described the scene, he reported that the Prince of Wales was kept in an apartment 'from which there was neither an entrance nor an exit except through the chamber of the king'. He lived under a degree of restraint more suited to a girl. 'He does not speak a word except in reply to what the king asks him.' He was unable to go out except through a private door that led into a park, and even then he was closely guarded.[15]

Henry VII's over-protectiveness was exacerbated by his worsening health and by rumours of renewed Yorkist conspiracy. After his wife's death, his hair whitened and his eyesight started to fail. When he lay sick for several weeks at his recently purchased hideaway manor of Wanstead in Essex – the exact date is unclear, but it was shortly after the new Prince of Wales's investiture – it was reported at Calais, the last of England's continental possessions and an important trading gateway, that 'the king's grace is but a weak man and sickly, not likely to be no long lived man'. According to John Flamank, one of the king's spies, there was much talk of who would succeed him 'if his grace happened to depart'. Some tipped the Duke of Buckingham, Edward IV's nephew and the country's richest peer, others Edmund de la Pole.[16] Strikingly, no one spoke of the younger Henry as the next king – as if the Tudor dynasty would die with its creator.

Obsessed with the need to prevent such a catastrophe, Henry VII had already arranged for his surviving son to be betrothed to Katherine of Aragon, Arthur's widow. On 25 June 1503, three days before Henry turned twelve, the ceremony had been held at the Bishop of Salisbury's palace in Fleet Street. Since, however, the age of consent to marriage for a girl was twelve and for a boy fourteen, the prospective bridegroom had the right to change his mind for another two years.[17]

The new marriage treaty contained many pitfalls, notably

a clause setting out the need first to secure a papal dispensation for the wedding, necessary since canon law forbade a man from marrying his brother's widow without one. Instead of recording Katherine's claim to be still a virgin when Arthur died (as later she vehemently maintained she was), the clause explained that her marriage to Arthur 'was solemnised according to the rites of the Catholic Church, and afterwards consummated'. From Henry VII's perspective, that was essential, since if there had been no consummation, there was no valid marriage, and thus he would be required to return Katherine's dowry to her father. Eager for his own reasons to expedite his daughter's remarriage, Ferdinand overlooked this. Writing to his ambassador in Rome that August, he said, 'As the English are much disposed to cavil, it has seemed to be more prudent to provide for the case as though the marriage had been consummated.'

But when after numerous delays Pope Julius II officially issued the bull of dispensation in 1504, he gave as his reason the need to foster peace between England and Spain, hedging his bets by saying that Katherine's first marriage was 'perhaps consummated'. Then, later, in a variant text of the dispensation supposedly sent to Spain and known as 'the brief', the wording was changed. Where the bull said that the dispensation was granted on grounds of peace, the brief said it was for this 'and other reasons'. Where the bull said that Katherine's first marriage had 'perhaps' been consummated, the brief stated unequivocally that it had been.[18] This confusion would later return to haunt Henry and Katherine.

The pope had first signalled his willingness to grant the

dispensation in the summer of 1504, after which a 'wedding' took place in which Henry and Katherine exchanged vows and promised to take each other 'as their lawful wedded spouse'. This bound her to him, but not he to her, since – unlike her – he was still under the age of consent. And of course the 'marriage' was not consummated – naturally, because, quite apart from the issue of his son's tender age, Henry VII's whole purpose was that his only male heir should most definitely remain uncommitted. This was how the savvy king extracted the maximum benefit from the Spanish alliance and retained Katherine's dowry, while keeping all his options open.[19]

And he had been wise, since the union of the crowns of Aragon and Castile was only a personal one. When Isabella of Castile, Katherine's mother, unexpectedly died that November, leaving Katherine's elder sister Juana as her heir, Spain was thrown into chaos. All depended on whether Ferdinand would be governor of the whole of Spain or whether Juana's husband, Philip the Handsome, Archduke of the Netherlands, Maximilian I's son, would seek to be more than a titular king of Castile.

Henry VII did not intend to persist with the marriage of his only surviving son to Katherine if he thought Castile and Aragon were about to break apart. In consequence, Prince Henry – on the eve of his fourteenth birthday and as part of his father's spider's web of diplomacy – read out a solemn protest before witnesses, repudiating his 'wedding'.

Now Henry VII scoured the courts of Europe for allies, beginning with Archduke Philip, who indeed planned to rule Castile in person. And when news arrived that Edmund de la Pole had entered Philip's dominions, he stepped up the pressure for his extradition. His opportunity came in January 1506, when a violent storm in the English Channel cast Philip and Juana ashore at Melcombe Regis in Dorset on their outward voyage from the Netherlands to Spain. Enticing Philip inland for an enforced stay, the elder Henry showered him with gifts and hospitality at Windsor Castle and Richmond Palace, and in return Philip agreed to extradite de la Pole on condition the English king solemnly swore that his life would be spared.[20]

During Philip's visit, the younger Henry acted as his co-host, greeting him at Winchester. There, he proudly took him on a visit to admire the vast wooden disc known as King Arthur's Round Table in the great hall of the castle. By this time, Henry had read the French chronicles of Jean le Bel and Jean Froissart that described in thrilling detail Edward III's fabled victory at Crécy and Henry V's at Agincourt during the Hundred Years War. He had eagerly devoured the tales of chivalry from the Arthurian romances, almost certainly from Sir Thomas Malory's *Le Morte D'Arthur* in William Caxton's printed edition of 1485, so laying down the foundations of his own claim to the throne of France.[21]

On arrival at Windsor, the teenage prince sat in on some of the secret conversations between Henry VII and Philip – it was almost as if he had become his father's apprentice. Their diplomacy reached its climax with the signing of a treaty of amity and an exchange of orders of chivalry, when Philip invested the prince with a golden collar, kissed him and made him a knight of the Order of the Golden Fleece.[22]

The twenty-seven-year-old Philip was a fine sportsman: as their encounter progressed, Prince Henry increasingly appeared to be captivated by him. In fact, the more Henry saw of Philip, the more he seemed to regard him as a hero. According to an eyewitness in Philip's entourage, from the moment the two first met, they had struck up an instant rapport – 'you'd be forced to conclude that they were brothers and good friends'.[23] Even twenty years later, it would be said that Henry never tired of talking of him.[24]

Within six months of landing in Spain, Philip was dead from an unexplained fever, but his influence lived on, for as soon as Henry's formal education ended on his sixteenth birthday, he began learning to joust. Bernard André – a blind court poet and one of Prince Arthur's old tutors – reported that while Henry VII was convalescing at Eltham after a severe bout of sickness in mid May 1508, his son was at nearby Greenwich, 'practising the first moves in warfare with his martial companions trained in the lists, and does so daily'.[25] By this, André meant that Henry was being allowed to 'run at the ring'. 'Running at the ring', while mounted on a stallion and wearing full armour, was the way young knights learned how to joust. Participants took turns to ride along the barrier in the tiltyard that divided the contestants in a real-life tournament, before taking aim with their lance at a ring suspended from a post that replaced the opponent in a genuine contest. Whoever speared the ring with his lance the most times after a set number of courses would be declared the winner.[26]

At the Whitsun jousts in June 1508, the Prince of Wales opened the proceedings by running at the ring 'supported by some very famous nobles'. The next month, he excelled himself again, this time at Richmond, watched anxiously by his father, 'when he surpassed all the rest'.[27] By now, said the Spanish ambassador, the young Henry was 'already taller than his father, and his limbs are of a gigantic size'.[28] Judging by the measurements of his earliest surviving suit of armour, there was some hyperbole here. Henry was at least 6 feet 2 inches tall, but as yet he had no more than a 42-inch chest measurement and a waistline of around 35 inches.

Increasingly paranoid about the succession after 1503, Henry VII also became avaricious, resented by the nobles and citizens of London for his extortions. Determined to silence his critics and clamp down on the families and networks of those he suspected, he unleashed two of his ablest apparatchiks, Richard Empson and Edmund Dudley, to construct an endemic culture of fear and coercion. As Dudley later explained, the king's 'pleasure and mind . . . was much set to have many persons in his danger at his pleasure'.[29]

Empson and Dudley were slick, ambitious lawyers, unquestioningly loyal and willing to cut corners. Under the king's vigilant supervision, they used a deadly combination of surveillance, blackmail, intimidation and threats to silence opposition even where it did not exist. Their activities split the King's Council, dividing the more ethically minded councillors against the more ruthless ones who helped themselves to a share of the spoils.

The ailing Henry VII's recurrent illnesses finally got the better of him. His mother, the redoubtable Lady Margaret Beaufort, moved to be near him as he lay dying at

Richmond. By 31 March 1509, he was said to be 'utterly without hope of recovery'. A week later, a scribe was paid for writing the king's last will, but he lingered on until 11 p.m. on Saturday 21 April.[30]

When Henry died, those closest to him kept his death secret for two days, fearing that the disaffection he had created would result in a dangerous backlash. A deal had first to be reached on behalf of the incoming king that Empson and Dudley would be made the scapegoats for his father's extortions.[31] Margaret Beaufort – still keeping vigil – may have urged on this deal, which had its origins in her dying son's conversations with his confessor.[32] So it was not until Monday 23 April that the old king's death was announced to the Court, and only next day did the heralds proclaim his son king.

As soon as the proclamation was made, the new king – still two months short of his eighteenth birthday – left Richmond for the Tower, where he surrounded himself with tight security for a month. During that time he took control of his father's treasure, and to court instant popularity confirmed, in amplified form, a general pardon granted by his father on his deathbed, inviting anyone with grievances against the old regime to lodge their petitions.[33]

Next, Henry began restoring to favour many of his mother's relatives who had fallen foul of his father, but not Edmund de la Pole and his brother. Among the beneficiaries – once suitable arrangements about their lands could be made – would be his mother's cousin Margaret Pole, Countess of Salisbury, and her sons Henry, Reginald and Geoffrey. Another prominent beneficiary would be Henry's cousin on his mother's side, the ten-year-old Henry Courtenay. When he finally came of age, Courtenay would become one of the young king's favourite jousting and gambling partners: appointed a gentleman of the Privy Chamber, he would also be elevated to the peerage as the Marquis of Exeter.[34]

But most astonishing to those around him was Henry's first major decision as king. Less than six weeks into his reign, he announced his intention of marrying Katherine of Aragon for a second time, overruling his older councillors, who warned that Ferdinand could prove a slippery ally and that the old papal bull of dispensation might be insufficient.[35] At one moment Henry claimed that he was deeply in love; at another that he was fulfilling his father's dying wishes.[36] Most likely, he believed that marrying Katherine was the fastest way to secure the dynasty and his throne. His father had drilled into him the need for dynasty security: Henry was already anxious for sons of his own and Katherine was royal, available and came of fecund stock.

On 11 June 1509, Henry and Katherine were quietly married in the Franciscan church at Greenwich, after which they were crowned in high pomp at Westminster Abbey on Midsummer's Day. And with his coronation safely behind him, Henry lost no time in having Empson and Dudley indicted on trumped-up treason charges. Empson was tried in his home county of Northamptonshire, where his predatory reputation guaranteed that the jurors would convict him; Dudley was tried in London for identical reasons. In both cases, their indictments falsely claimed that they had called up armed men to London to seize and kill the new king, whereas in reality they had merely mustered their bodyguards for their own protection.[37] None of the old king's other bureaucrats were punished – on the contrary, they flocked to avail themselves of the general pardon.

Henry then bided his time for almost another year, diverting himself (as he told his father-in-law, Ferdinand) by 'jousting, hawking, hunting and other innocent and honest pastimes' and by 'visiting different parts of the kingdom'.[38] He kept Empson and Dudley alive, locked away in the Tower, in case they still had information useful to him. Then, utterly impatient with the barrage of petitions for redress of grievances he had invited, he decided to silence criticism once and for all by killing them.[39]

Neither Empson nor Dudley was a traitor. But Henry sacrificed them to ensure his smooth accession, and both were beheaded while he rode out hunting. If his grandmother had chiefly urged on their arrests, one might argue that she ought to share the blame for their deaths. But she died five days after her grandson's coronation, before Empson and Dudley were even put on trial.

Henry alone, therefore, shoulders the responsibility for judicially murdering two of his father's most trusted ministers, however much he attempted to evade it by pretending they were guilty of serious crimes. It would prove to be the earliest indication of his deadly impatience in the face of knotty problems as well as of the sort of sudden, deeply personal revulsion that in later years would lead him to commit a series of similar acts of callous expediency. Few kings of England were more ready to reclassify friends and loyal servants as traitors if they disappointed him.[40]

2

The Pope's Loyal Son

From the outset, Henry VIII meant to make a splash in war and foreign affairs. His councillors recommended that he renew without delay the old king's peace treaties with France and its ally Scotland, but for months Henry stubbornly resisted them.[1] With all the ardour of youth, he dreamed of emulating the legendary Henry V, leading his army across the Channel to claim the French throne, and of helping Ferdinand to expel the French from Italy.[2] It was not a matter of whether but of when he would muster his forces.

As a young man, Henry would also be an eager champion of the papacy, even supplying Cornish tin for roofing works at Pope Julius II's new basilica of St Peter's in Rome.[3] With French armies on the rampage in Italy, he sent an envoy to Paris to urge Louis XII to make peace with the pope 'on terms which the pope considered just'.[4] When the envoy reported that the French king's response had been to summon a schismatic General Council of the Church at Pisa in May 1511 with a view to deposing Julius, Henry was scandalized. War with France was inevitable.[5]

In 1512, Henry sent an expensively equipped force under the command of the Marquis of Dorset by sea to Aquitaine.

Then, the following year, he personally led an even larger army into northern France, intending to march into Normandy. Dorset's expedition was a fiasco – Henry was betrayed by the perfidious Ferdinand, whose only interest was in conquering for himself the independent kingdom of Navarre on the frontier of France and Spain. Henry's own campaign had more success. Although nothing came of the king's plan to invade Normandy, his troops, assisted by those of his ally Maximilian I, besieged and captured the towns of Thérouanne and Tournai (both then in French territory), chasing away the French and enabling Henry to claim that he had won a glorious victory.[6]

William Warham, the Archbishop of Canterbury, was strongly opposed to the war, but Henry would not listen. He had been offered an alluring incentive by Pope Julius, who had officially stripped Louis of his papal title of 'Most Christian King' and promised it – along with the kingdom of France itself – to Henry, who was offered the mouth-watering prospect of a coronation in Paris, perhaps at the hands of the pope himself. Naturally, there were conditions. Henry had to keep France forever 'in faith, devotion and obedience to the Holy Roman Church and Apostolic See'. He also had to defeat Louis in battle. A measure of Henry's desperation for recognition as well as his naivety as a twenty-one-year-old is that he was bewitched by such blarney. When Julius died in 1513, however, the new pope, Leo X, feigned ignorance of the offer.[7]

Henry did have something to boast about after James IV of Scotland threatened him. Henry VII had married his elder daughter, Margaret, to James as part of a peace accord, but seeing an opportunity to steal a march on his brother-in-law while the latter was away in France, James crossed the frontier with an army. Like his royal predecessors, Henry VIII claimed to be the Scottish king's feudal overlord. In order to humble James, he ordered Thomas Howard, Earl of Surrey (later Duke of Norfolk), across the River Tweed with an army. In atrocious weather at the Battle of Flodden on 9 September 1513, and on soaking, slippery ground, Surrey's men killed James and a large proportion of his nobility in a bloody battle, leaving Henry's sister as the regent in Scotland during a long royal minority.

Otherwise, the sole beneficiary of Henry's early wars was the forty-two-year-old Thomas Wolsey, an Oxford-educated butcher's son from Ipswich who had masterminded the procurement of troops and military supplies, and was rewarded with the bishopric of Lincoln. By the summer of 1514, Henry was lobbying Pope Leo to make Wolsey a cardinal. And when the archbishopric of York fell unexpectedly vacant, Wolsey quickly secured it.

One of Henry VII's lesser apparatchiks in the closing years of his reign, Wolsey had risen to prominence as the new king's favourite councillor. Swiftly outclassing all potential rivals, he was said to be the 'most earnest and readiest ... to advance the King's only will and pleasure without any respect to the case'. A man with no guiding political principles, he had instead a will to serve the king and to succeed, combined with 'a special gift of natural eloquence with a filed tongue to pronounce the same, that he was able with the same to persuade and allure all men to his purpose'.[8] Whenever he wanted something urgently from

Henry, noted a visiting Italian, Wolsey would introduce the topic casually into the conversation. He then brought out some small gift – a ring or jewel, or a beautifully crafted silver dish – and while Henry was admiring it, 'would adroitly bring forward the project on which his mind was fixed'.[9]

Wolsey's challenge was to position Henry in the premier league of European princes, putting him in the same hall of fame as the English heroes he had read about as an adolescent in the Arthurian romances and French chronicles. Glory in war and magnificence in peace were Henry's chief aims. War, however, could be ruinously expensive. Peace, argued Wolsey, had the advantage: it could be just as glorious – but was much cheaper.

Using agents in Rome whom he systematically recruited and carefully nurtured alongside members of his own entourage, Wolsey first brokered an Anglo-French rapprochement under which Henry's younger sister, the eighteen-year-old Mary, was married to the fifty-two-year-old French king, Louis XII. The peace was intended to last until at least a year after the death of whichever ruler died first and Henry was to receive a generous French 'pension', paid annually, that he interpreted as 'tribute' from his kingdom of France.

Louis, 'licking his lips and gulping his spittle' at the mere sight of his pretty young bride, was 'very joyous' after his wedding night. But within twelve weeks he was dead, enabling his widow secretly to marry her true love, Charles Brandon, Duke of Suffolk, her brother's favourite jousting companion.[10]

With the coming of the new French king, the twenty-year-old Francis I, the Anglo-French peace did not last long. In 1515 Francis led his army across the Alps to win a spectacular victory at the Battle of Marignano, reigniting French ambitions in northern Italy. Unsure how to react, Henry turned to Pope Leo for advice and guidance. And to make sure the pope did not miss his cue, Wolsey dropped the broadest of hints that he should grant Henry a title 'that shall be ascribed to his perpetual memory and chronicled amongst other his noble deeds'.[11] Two months earlier, in front of visiting Venetian ambassadors, Henry had emphasized his undying loyalty to the pope: 'I am the pope's good son, and will always be with his holiness and with the Church, from which I mean never to depart.' Evidently, though, the relationship was meant to be reciprocal, for Henry also confided, 'I think I have sufficient power with the pope to warrant hopes of my making him adhere to whichever side I choose.'[12]

It was a disarming comment, showing that – if Henry believed it to be true – he already had delusions of grandeur.

On 10 September 1515, Henry's lobbying bore at least partial fruit when Wolsey was elected a cardinal; on Christmas Eve he also replaced William Warham as Lord Chancellor. From now on, Henry, although twenty years younger than Wolsey, declared him to be his friend: he would link arms with him as they strolled together in the king's privy garden. He wrote letters to him in his own hand rather than simply dictating them to a secretary, which he otherwise did only when writing to foreign princes. Such tokens of

Henry's esteem were a clear signal that Wolsey had become the king's chief minister and was not to be trifled with. Foreign ambassadors called him an 'alter rex' or 'second king'.[13]

'Mine own good cardinal,' Henry began a letter to Wolsey in 1518, 'I recommend me unto you with all my heart, and thank you for the great pain and labour that you do daily take in my business and matters.' Another that year opened in similar vein: 'My Lord Cardinal, I recommend unto you as heartily as I can, and I am right glad to hear of your good health.'[14]

The last was no idle remark, for Henry was a lifelong hypochondriac – he even devised his own prophylactic against plague involving red briar and elder leaves, ginger and copious quantities of white wine.[15] Early in 1514, he had been laid low with what some said was measles and others an attack of smallpox, and in 1518 the sweating sickness – a viral pulmonary disease – had returned to London.[16] To his extreme consternation, the pages sleeping on pallets outside his bedchamber at Richmond Palace were struck down.[17] To escape danger, he fled to the safety of rural Oxfordshire. Even Wolsey was forbidden to visit until the scare was over, since the cardinal had succumbed to the deadly virus the previous summer and was among the few who lived to tell the tale.[18]

Henry allowed Wolsey unusual freedom, especially in domestic affairs: indeed, the two would first decide policy between themselves, and only after they had done so would they consult the rest of the King's Council.[19] Sometimes Henry would tease his chief minister that he worked too hard and should take some 'pastime and comfort to the intent you may the longer endure to serve us, for always pain cannot be endured'.[20]

Despite often displaying his alarmingly low threshold of boredom, Henry considered himself an expert on the work–life balance. In the summer he spent whole days hunting or hawking. One of his secretaries, Richard Pace, told Wolsey sardonically, 'The king rises daily, except on holy days, at 4 or 5 o'clock and hunts till 9 or 10 at night. He spares no pains to convert the sport of hunting into a martyrdom.'[21] Otherwise, Henry spent his mornings jousting, shooting from a stand, horse racing or playing at bowls or tennis and his evenings dancing or gambling at cards or shuffleboard – but despite this he kept a close watching brief over affairs.

In 1518, Wolsey found an ingenious way to put Henry's name on the lips of every ruler in Christendom.[22] He first persuaded him to sell Tournai back to Francis and make a new Anglo-French alliance. Then, when Pope Leo unveiled a plan for a general European truce and a crusade against the Ottoman Turks, he hijacked the diplomacy, turning it into a dazzling Treaty of Universal Peace, making London the hub of pan-European affairs and Henry the arbiter of international disputes under the blessing of the pope. Since every European ruler who mattered to Henry was a party to the treaty, it was just bad luck that the Holy Roman Emperor, Maximilian I, died a year later. Wolsey sought to remedy the situation by courting Maximilian's successor, Charles V, Katherine of Aragon's nineteen-year-old nephew, with a view to a fresh treaty. But the odds were stacked against him. Already King of Spain after Ferdinand's death in 1516, Charles – with his calculating mind and far greater resources of manpower and money – had shifted the balance of power and had no intention of making himself answerable to Henry.

Wolsey, in 1520, contrived to keep Henry centre stage by organizing a personal interview between him and Francis in the so-called 'Golden Valley' halfway between the towns of Guisnes and Ardres, near Calais. A celebration of the two kings' cultural tastes as much as of their power and sporting prowess, the 'Field of Cloth of Gold' (as it came to be known) was a glittering chivalric extravaganza lasting more than a fortnight, complete with fairytale banquets, masques, tournaments and displays of art treasures.[23] As a signal of his even-handedness, before leaving for France, Henry met the young Holy Roman Emperor, Charles, at Canterbury: they knelt together at the shrine of Thomas Becket and kissed a relic of the True Cross. And, after returning from the Golden Valley, he met Charles again at Gravelines and Calais.[24]

Through these encounters, Henry came to believe he was far more important in European affairs than he really was. Wolsey's talent for pulling rabbits out of hats showed not just his diplomatic genius but a deep understanding of the fame and recognition for which Henry yearned.

By now, Henry was in his prime, 'as handsome as nature could form him' as a visiting Venetian described him: 'handsomer by far than the King of France'.[25] 'Exceedingly fair' and with thick auburn hair, his neck was long and thick, his fingers studded with jewelled rings and around his neck he wore a gold collar from which hung a diamond 'the size of the largest walnut I ever saw and to this was suspended a most beautiful and very large round pearl'.[26] A ruler blessed with many talents, honed by his boyhood tutors, he was already known to be a keen amateur student of astronomy, geometry and theology and would within a few years become something of an expert on maps, fortifications and the royal navy.[27] His only flaw, it was said, was that he 'could not abide to have any man stare in his face or to fix his eye too steadily upon him when he talked with them'.[28]

But he did not yet have a male heir, and that was starting to trouble him.

After miscarrying in January 1510, Katherine of Aragon had given birth to a boy on the following New Year's Day, delighting Henry. To offer thanks, he went on a pilgrimage to the shrine of the Virgin Mary at Walsingham in Norfolk and commissioned two days of magnificent jousts in the tiltyard at Westminster.[29] But when just seven weeks old, the child died.[30] Pregnant at least four more times over the next eight years, Katherine would have two more stillborn children as well as another boy who died shortly after birth.

Two modern medical experts hypothesize that Katherine's pregnancy failures were caused by haemolytic disease of the newborn, arising from a rare incompatibility of one of Henry's minor blood group antigens with hers.[31] In 1516, she had a healthy daughter, christened Mary, but for Henry this would not do: England had never had a woman ruler before, and for a society that was patriarchal to the core, the idea was almost unthinkable. If Mary went on to be queen and if, as queen, she married – as surely she must if the dynasty were to survive – the problem as Henry saw it would be compounded, because her husband would demand to be king.[32]

Katherine's gynaecological difficulties encouraged Henry's serial infidelities.[33] After she miscarried in 1514, he was overheard cruelly taunting and reproaching her.[34] And in 1519, he proved to his own satisfaction his ability to father healthy sons when Elizabeth Blount, his current mistress, gave birth to a boy, whom he acknowledged from the start and named Henry 'Fitzroy' or 'king's son'.

In February 1521, Henry returned with Katherine to Walsingham on a pilgrimage driven by her desire to conceive a living son before she entered the menopause. But barely was Henry within sight of the town than, suddenly suspecting treason, he turned in his tracks and rode back alone to Essex.[35] Then, alerted to imminent danger by Wolsey, he hastened onwards to Greenwich, where he planned to strike against the Duke of Buckingham.

Ever since his mother had been forced to snatch him from his nursery and rush with him to the safety of the Tower shortly before he was six, Henry had been fearful of suspected Yorkist conspiracy. Before embarking for Calais with his army in 1513, he had Edmund de la Pole brought out of the Tower and beheaded – this despite Henry VII's oath to spare Edmund's life. In 1516, Henry had even been behind a clumsy attempt to assassinate Edmund's brother, Richard, then in France.[36] When, in 1518, the king's fears briefly returned, he scribbled a hasty note to Wolsey disclosing his doubts about a group of prominent nobles, chiefly the Duke of Buckingham, already tipped in Henry VII's reign as a possible claimant to the throne.[37]

Nothing came of the incident at the time, but in mid-April 1521, Buckingham was arrested with his son-in-law, Lord Bergavenny, whose loyalty had been in doubt as long ago as 1497 when he had been surprised in bed with Edmund de la Pole.[38] Bergavenny was exonerated, but Buckingham charged with high treason. His indictment claimed that he had 'imagined and compassed' Henry's deposition and death during conversations with Nicholas Hopkins, a Carthusian monk. More credibly, he stood accused of slandering Wolsey.[39]

At his trial, Buckingham cried foul, for Henry had personally coached the witnesses, such was his burning desire for a conviction. Beheaded by a bungling headsman who took three strokes of the axe to cleave through the sinews of his neck, Buckingham was a victim of Henry's sense of insecurity caused by his lack of a legitimate male heir. The duke had been foolish to listen to Hopkins, but was no traitor, merely a vain, proud nobleman who resented the way in which he had been sidelined.[40]

Beginning with Empson and Dudley and continuing throughout his life, Henry would refuse to confront or grant an audience to those he was intent on destroying. His sudden evasiveness as evidenced by his inability to hold a person's gaze was as much a defect of his character as his suspiciousness. Nor would he attend the executions of those whose deaths he could spend days or weeks planning – although in Buckingham's case, he would have been prevented by a particularly severe bout of tertian fever. To mark his recovery, he went on a pilgrimage to the shrine of

John Schorne, a popular English saint, at North Marston in Buckinghamshire, which he had visited once before in 1511.[41] There, he prayed and made an offering in thanks to God, returning to Richmond feeling fitter than for several months – and eager to resume a task into which he was throwing himself with more than his usual gusto.

In the same month that Buckingham was arrested, Henry had been reading *De Captivitate Babylonica Ecclesiae* ('The Babylonian Captivity of the Church'), published the previous year, by the rebel German monk Martin Luther. Deeply affronted by Luther's attacks on papal power, Church indulgences and claims that only three of the seven Catholic sacraments had been instituted by Christ, opinions all of which he considered to be heretical, Henry decided to complete a project he had first tentatively begun three years before, taking up his pen to defend the pope and the Catholic faith in a book entitled *Assertio Septem Sacramentorum* ('A Defence of the Seven Sacraments').[42] To help him complete his manuscript and make it ready for publication, he conscripted Thomas More, since 1518 his principal secretary. When More cautiously warned Henry that, while attacking Luther's opinions of the sacraments was wholly to be applauded, it might be prudent to tone down his own unqualified defence of papal power in case he quarrelled with the pope in the future, the king refused. 'We received from that See our crown imperial,' he reputedly said, and 'We are so much bounden unto the See of Rome that we cannot do too much honour unto it.'[43] To illustrate his point, Henry signed his name on the frontispiece of a presentation copy of his book, dedicated to Pope Leo and bound in cloth of gold. There, an illuminated miniature directly above his signature depicts him wearing a closed or 'imperial' crown and kneeling before the pope to receive a blessing.[44]

On the arrival of the book in Rome and at Wolsey's further urging, Henry at last received the papal title he had coveted since the first years of his reign – though it was not given purely on account of the book.[45] Not awarded until October 1521, the title would be withheld until Henry had also committed himself to allying with the pope and Charles V as the prelude to a fresh attempt to expel the French from Italy. When first sounded out by Wolsey about the new alliance, Henry had revived his claim to the title of 'Most Christian King' promised by the former pope, Julius II. He was not yet sure that he had the stomach for another costly war and knew his subjects would resent the taxes needed to pay for it. But when Charles promised to hunt down and extradite from France 'all usurpers' (including exiled Yorkists) and, with Leo, proposed a partition of the country in which the English king received the lion's share of the spoils, Henry agreed, provided the pope conceded the title. The outcome was a compromise in which the pope awarded Henry the alternative title of 'Defender of the Faith'.[46]

In June 1522, the allies ratified their commitment to what they called their 'Great Enterprise' against France, Charles and Henry, wearing identical clothes, riding side by side in triumph through the streets of London. And to cement their friendship, Charles promised to marry his six-year-old cousin – Henry and Katherine's daughter Mary – when she reached the age of twelve.[47]

Leo, meanwhile, had died of a chill caught while sitting up late to celebrate the expulsion of the French from Milan. The new pope, Adrian VI – Charles's old tutor and, during his childhood, regent of Spain – was a peacemaker, hence a stalemate ensued between Francis, Henry and Charles until France's most powerful nobleman, the Duke of Bourbon, offered to rebel against Francis. For Henry it seemed to be a golden opportunity. In late August 1523, as soon as a treaty between Henry, Bourbon and Charles could be signed, Wolsey began shipping a large army across the Channel under the command of the king's brother-in-law the Duke of Suffolk.[48]

To Henry's dismay, Bourbon's revolt catastrophically misfired and, after an encouraging start, Suffolk's march on Paris ended in abject failure.[49] Following these twin humiliations, Henry's commitment to the Great Enterprise dramatically waned, especially when his cash reserves were spent.

Papal policy took a further backward step, as far as Henry was concerned, when Giulio de' Medici succeeded as Pope Clement VII, Adrian having died of kidney disease during Suffolk's march on Paris. Throughout the following year, the new pope sought to remain neutral, even when Henry – against Wolsey's advice – financed Bourbon in a misguided attempt to besiege Marseilles. Then, early in 1525, the new pope buckled. Francis had crossed the Alps again and laid siege to Pavia, also sending a force south towards Naples. Fearing that Rome would be encircled, Clement, casting his policy of neutrality to the winds, impulsively allied with Francis against Charles.[50]

Henry was about to join him in this spectacular act of misjudgement when, in February that year, news arrived of Charles's triumph at the Battle of Pavia: Francis had been captured and his army wiped out.[51] The body of Richard de la Pole, the Yorkist exile who had fought at Pavia for Francis, was found where he had fallen – news that gave Henry double cause for jubilation.

On hearing that Francis had been taken prisoner, Henry rejoiced all the more and sought to revive the Great Enterprise without delay. 'Now is the time,' he enthused to visiting diplomats, 'for the emperor and myself to devise the means of getting full satisfaction from France. Not an hour is to be lost.'[52] But Charles's victory was complete: he ordered Francis to be taken in chains to Madrid and refused to listen further to Henry. Anxious to stop fighting, for he too was now running low on cash, Charles even ditched his engagement to Mary Tudor, marrying instead his cousin Isabella, the Infanta of Portugal. An indignant Henry countered that not only did he expect to be restored to the role of arbitrator of Christendom he had briefly played after the Treaty of Universal Peace, but that he expected Charles to send the captured Francis to England. Alternatively, Henry wanted Charles to meet him in Paris and watch him being crowned King of France.[53]

When his shrill demands were ignored by Charles, Henry, believing himself betrayed, renounced his erstwhile allies – including Pope Clement, who with Charles in command of Italy had in effect become the emperor's vassal. His disenchantment knowing no bounds, Henry authorized Wolsey to make a separate peace with France, breaking with the habit of a lifetime by declining to consult Rome first.[54] Clement was thunderstruck: no longer was Henry to be relied on as 'the pope's good son'. But Henry was unmoved. Already thirty-four and more experienced in the pitfalls of European affairs, he was beginning to assert himself. Less open to advice or criticism than he had been earlier, he adopted a more hectoring style, even with Wolsey. Now, Henry was prepared to slap down his chief minister if he thought he had stepped out of line.[55]

By the mid 1520s, Katherine of Aragon had lost her figure and grown fat. Turning forty in 1525, she had also passed the menopause, making Charles's decision to jilt Mary a double blow. While his daughter's engagement was still on, Henry held out the prospect that the English succession might pass to Mary and Charles.[56] After it was broken off, he summoned his illegitimate son, Fitzroy, to Court and invested him as Duke of Richmond and Somerset.[57] These were royal titles: Henry's grandfather, Edmund Tudor, had been first Earl of Richmond, while the dukedom of Somerset descended from Henry's Beaufort ancestors. The investiture was thus a signal that Fitzroy's succession was an option on the table; it might perhaps have remained so had not Fitzroy died as a teenager from the complications of bronchial pneumonia.

When precisely Henry decided to divorce Katherine is unclear. In 1522 he was bedding Mary Boleyn, the daughter of one of his leading courtiers, Sir Thomas Boleyn.[58] Their affair became public when Henry named a royal navy ship after her.[59] When he dropped her is uncertain, but it was most likely in the summer of 1525.

It was during the following year that he fell in love with Mary's sister, Anne. A brunette with a dark complexion in an age when a fair complexion was generally preferred, her looks were considered unremarkable, but as a gentlewoman for seven years to Francis I's wife, Queen Claude, she had French *chic*.[60] Self-confident and outspoken, and a convert to the viewpoint of the evangelical religious reformers in Paris whose books – as well as the Bible – she read avidly in French, she stood out from the crowd. After Henry had declared his love for her, she dared to think that, although a commoner, she might one day be worthy to be his wife, rather than his mistress.[61]

When Anne refused to sleep with him, Henry was at first curious, then piqued. Women did not normally refuse him. Could it be that she did not really love him? In an extraordinary series of passionate love letters Henry wrote to Anne, there was, slipped between the outpourings of his heart, the occasional veiled threat: his patience, he said, was limited. She had to decide.[62]

In the end, however, he gave in and agreed to her terms. With Henry madly in love with her and refusing to believe that God could deny him the son on whom he had set his heart, Anne played her trump card, vowing to give him a male heir, one who – unlike Fitzroy – could be certain to be legitimate, because his parents would be married.

Henry naively imagined that an annulment of his marriage to Katherine would be straightforward. There were ample precedents to this effect: among them, Louis XII of France had divorced his wife to marry Anne of Brittany, and Henry's own sister Margaret, the widow of James IV, had managed to have her second marriage dissolved.

In April 1527, Henry informed Wolsey in confidence of his deep 'scruples' about the validity of his marriage, but to spare himself embarrassment concealed from him his intention to make Anne his queen. By taking this evasive approach, he hamstrung Wolsey from the outset.

Henry's argument was that the papal bull of dispensation secured by his father from Pope Julius II in 1504, granting him permission to marry his deceased brother's widow, was in contravention of Scripture and should never have been issued. He maintained that he and Katherine were living in sin, on account of which God had denied him living sons by her. Henry therefore asked Wolsey in his capacity as a leading churchman to 'examine' his case and 'cleanse' his conscience by arranging a divorce.

By this time, Charles had released Francis from captivity, but the French king broke their agreement and was absolved by Pope Clement, who hastily assembled the League of Cognac – made up of him, France and the leading Italian city states – to oppose Charles's domination of Italy. To the pope's deep chagrin, Henry refused to join the League as a full member. Feeling he had been cheated too often by his former allies, he was now less interested in Italian affairs than in his pursuit of Anne and the most he was willing to offer Clement was a subsidy.[63]

When Henry had first told Wolsey of his scruples and asked him for a divorce, his chief minister was attempting to pull chestnuts out of the fire in the shape of another pan-European peace accord along the lines of the Treaty of Universal Peace of 1518. His plans turned to ashes in May 1527, when Charles's army in Italy under the command of the ubiquitous Duke of Bourbon mutinied and sacked Rome, forcing Pope Clement to flee from the Vatican through a secret tunnel to the Castel Sant' Angelo, where he signed a truce making himself Charles's prisoner.

Henry's response was to make a deeper commitment to the Anglo-French alliance. Ably assisted by Thomas More, whom Henry had promoted to the post of Chancellor of the Duchy of Lancaster, Wolsey rushed off to Amiens to confer with Francis, where terms were ratified and Henry's daughter Mary pledged in marriage to Francis's younger son. Afterwards, in a separate conference at Compiègne, Wolsey and Francis schemed to convene a powerful group of cardinals at Avignon and take over the government of the entire Church, claiming that the pope had been incapacitated by forces beyond his control. Thus empowered, Wolsey would be free both to pursue the cause of peace in Europe and settle Henry's divorce.[64]

Or would he? Henry, as impatient as ever when confronted with a knotty problem, was determined to have his divorce by fair means or foul and had already sent his new secretary, William Knight, to Rome behind Wolsey's back, to seek the necessary dispensations for him to marry Anne.[65] By 1527, Henry's fidelity to Wolsey was wavering and he was actively seeking to bypass his chief minister's carefully managed networks at the papal curia. Constantly shadowing Henry's and Wolsey's moves, meanwhile, were Anne's relatives – notably, her father Thomas, brother George and their allies – biding their time and poised to pounce.

A violent change was about to take place not just in Henry's private life and attitude to the pope and Church, but in his working habits and beliefs about kingship and authority. What once he had taken for granted, he was now prepared to challenge, even to overthrow. It was just a matter of time before he ceased for ever to be the pope's loyal son.

3
A Man of Conscience

In June 1527, Henry told Katherine of Aragon that their marriage was over. He reduced her to floods of tears by brusquely informing her that 'they had been in mortal sin in all the years they had lived together'.[1] Thereafter, his campaign to marry Anne Boleyn had dramatic effects on his outlook. As he repeatedly insisted, the scruples he had already disclosed to Wolsey about his first marriage had stirred his conscience, which meant he felt he had to satisfy God, rather than the pope.

He explained these scruples more fully to Thomas More, whom he was determined to win over to his side. Shortly after More had returned from Amiens in mid-October, Henry laid open the Book of Leviticus before him and pointed to a passage which he claimed prohibited marriage to a dead brother's wife:

> If a man shall take his brother's wife, it is an impurity. He hath uncovered his brother's nakedness: they shall be childless. (Leviticus 20:21)

As Henry argued, this was God's law: a law that no pope could dispense. He dismissed out of hand a contradictory text from the Book of Deuteronomy, claiming that it described a Jewish tradition known as the 'levirate' by which the brother or next of kin to a deceased man was bound, if unmarried, to marry the widow. This, he declared, was merely an ancient custom of the Jewish people, not binding on Christians.[2] To 'prove' these contentions, he had written another book. The earliest drafts and a polished version survive, showing that he had summoned experts to assist him, of whom the most important was Edward Foxe, Provost of King's College, Cambridge.[3]

Henry's Damascene moment had come in the middle of August 1527, when he had consulted a Hebrew expert at Cambridge, who interpreted the divine retribution threatened against illicit marriage partners according to Leviticus – 'they shall be childless' – as meaning 'they shall not have *sons*'.[4] But Henry went further, claiming that sexual intercourse with a brother's wife was incest pure and simple, and 'in such high degree against the law of nature'. It was, said More when told of it, 'the first time that ever I heard that point moved'.[5] And it lay at the heart of Henry's mental shift, because, within eighteen months, he would come to think that he was called by God to cleanse his sin, even if this meant resisting the pope. His conscience, he said, had been aroused, forcing him to take matters into his own hands. But Henry's was an elastic, self-serving view of conscience – and one diametrically opposed to the Catholic Church's teaching.[6]

Meanwhile, Wolsey's ingenious attempt at Compiègne to take over the government of the Church had failed, as for that matter had Knight's mission.[7] Equally futile was another plan, devised by an increasingly desperate Wolsey, to consider the king's case under the auspices of the papacy, in which he would sit jointly with Cardinal Lorenzo Campeggi. The choice of Campeggi, at first sight, was inspired. A stout partisan of England, he had been close to Wolsey since 1518, and had been appointed absentee Bishop of Salisbury for his services to Henry in Rome. When, however, the gout-stricken papal envoy arrived in London, he discovered to his horror just how inflexible Henry could be. So convinced of the righteousness of his cause was this king, Campeggi reported to the pope's secretary, that 'I believe an angel descending from heaven would be unable to persuade him otherwise'.[8]

Campeggi was doing all he could to delay a hearing of the case, when Katherine unexpectedly produced the variant text of Pope Julius's original dispensation of 1504, known as 'the brief', saying it had recently been discovered in Spain. According to documents now in the Vatican, she also claimed to have new evidence to prove she was a virgin after she married Arthur, including depositions concerning the inspection of the bed linen of Arthur and of Henry himself.[9] Although Campeggi had his doubts, and in Rome it was believed that none of this 'evidence' was conclusive in law, he was able to make the excuse that, in the light of its 'discovery', his commission to hear the case was invalid.

While Campeggi dragged his heels, Henry kept up his campaign in Rome, bribing cardinals and even threatening the pope. At length, on 31 May 1529, Wolsey joined Campeggi in the great hall at Blackfriars, a Dominican monastery beside the Thames in the heart of London, to begin a hearing of Henry's suit. At one of the court's sessions Henry, seated beneath a canopy of cloth of gold, put his case in person. When he had finished, Katherine made her impassioned defence, falling on her knees before Henry and begging him to consider her honour, her daughter's and his own.

But all was in vain. Even as the court began its hearings, a letter was on its way from Clement, bidding Campeggi to exploit every tactic of delay. And after wavering for six weeks, Clement – under constant pressure from Katherine's nephew Charles V – acceded to Katherine's plea that the case should be revoked to Rome.[10]

Wolsey, like lesser men in his position, discovered his fate only from gloating rivals. His last interview with Henry was on 19 September 1529 at Grafton in Northamptonshire, where he was courteously, if coolly, received, then denied a bed for the night.[11] Ordered on 11 October by the Dukes of Norfolk and Suffolk to surrender his seal of office, he was put under house arrest at Esher and summoned to appear at the Court of King's Bench.[12] There he was charged with *praemunire*, the offence of illegally bringing papal jurisdiction into England. He wisely pleaded guilty, was sentenced to life imprisonment and had all his property confiscated. In return for his co-operation, Henry sent him tokens – one a ring set with a ruby – along with a gnomic message that he 'was not angry with him in his heart'.[13] Retaining some personal affection for his fallen chief minister, Henry blocked treason charges in Parliament and spared Wolsey the indignity of imprisonment, allowing him to retire on conditions to his province of York.

Unfortunately for him, Wolsey misinterpreted these mixed messages. Believing there was still some hope of rehabilitation if he could somehow secure the king's divorce, he made clandestine overtures to Rome, Charles V and the French. After his ciphered messages were intercepted by royal agents, he was summoned back to London to face new charges and died of dysentery on the journey south.[14]

Henry chose Thomas More to be his new Lord Chancellor and – once More had accepted – was more pressing than ever in his attempt to win him over to the divorce; but More excused himself. As he later explained, the king 'graciously declared unto me ... that I should perceive mine own conscience should serve me, and that I should first look unto God and after God unto him'.[15]

Henry's willingness to respect other people's consciences would not last long. Soon, Anne Boleyn moved permanently into apartments near to his at Court, and under her influence he came to feel a sweeping emotional revulsion towards Katherine, exiling his rejected spouse from Court and then denying her access to her beloved daughter.[16] Always prone to sudden evasiveness when his fidelity to people and institutions turned to total and usually vengeful disenchantment, he now spoke to his former wife through intermediaries rather than confronting her face to face. He also withheld crucial information from Katherine, humiliating her by letting her first discover it from third parties.

Anne, meanwhile, was largely responsible for refocusing Henry's strategy on the divorce. In a concerted effort to break the deadlock, she persuaded him to allow her father, Sir Thomas, and brother George to send him fresh recruits to assist Edward Foxe. She even boldly showed him selected passages from the writings of William Tyndale, an English Lutheran and Bible translator who had fled abroad to escape a charge of heresy and was now living in Antwerp. She had reputedly marked the paragraphs she showed to Henry with her fingernail by pressing it hard on to the paper.[17]

Foxe's new team included a rising star from Cambridge, a theologian and New Testament scholar named Thomas Cranmer. By September 1530, Foxe and Cranmer had put before Henry a dossier showing (as they said) the 'true difference between royal and ecclesiastical power'. Its logic was devastatingly simple: the pope was no more than the 'bishop of Rome' – his jurisdiction limited to his own diocese – whereas the King of England was 'God's Vicar on Earth'. Accountable to Christ alone and imbued with quasi-'priestly' powers, Henry was supreme in his dominions: clergy and laity alike were subject to him. Should he choose to, he might define the articles of faith for his subjects, interpret the Bible and reform or suppress the monasteries. He might, more immediately, empower the Archbishop of Canterbury to investigate his scruples of conscience.

According to the dossier, Henry stood at a turning point of history. In the reign of William the Conqueror, it had been kings, not popes, who were superior in their realms – who appointed bishops and took order for the reform of the Church. Then, between the twelfth and fourteenth centuries, pontiffs such as Innocent III and Boniface VIII had proclaimed themselves superior to temporal princes, claiming that St Peter himself had given them a controlling authority over the government of Church and State.

The dossier made it plain that space now existed for a heroic figure who could confound such blatant 'usurpations' and 'restore' the true dignity and regality of kings, and especially the kings of England. Henry should reclaim for himself the 'just jurisdiction' of which he had been deprived by the papacy and declare himself without delay to be Christ's deputy on earth.[18]

Foxe's dossier still survives, complete with Henry's approving annotations marked in forty-six places. In compiling it, Foxe and his team provided the complete intellectual justification for a break with the papacy, and in the process showed their sure grasp of Henry's psychology. By offering him what he took to be written 'proof' that he was Christ's deputy on earth, they reignited his quest for fame.[19]

In January 1531, Henry demanded that the English bishops and senior clergy pay him an astronomical fine of £118,000 (£118 million in modern values) for so-called abuses of power and recognize him as 'Supreme Head and Sole Protector of the English Church'. Seeing their peril, they paid the fine and, after some haggling, declared the king to be 'Supreme Head of the English Church *as far as the law of Christ allows*' – a crucial qualification.[20] Pressure in this vein continued for another year, with the result that Thomas More resigned the chancellorship.[21] But it would take Henry at least two more years to act fully on Foxe's blueprint from the time he received it. When he did so, the result would be revolutionary, but until then, for all his infatuation with Anne, his heart still hankered for the old order. The fact that he had quarrelled with Rome and disobeyed

Pope Clement's advice to take back his wife had not yet over-come his gut allegiance to the universal Catholic Church.

The chain of events precipitating Henry's break with Rome began in October 1532 with an Anglo-French summit, arranged to ratify a new Treaty of Mutual Aid. Masterminded by the Boleyns and Edward Foxe, the treaty was designed to mobilize French support in Rome for the divorce and was seen as a diplomatic triumph.[22] After Henry and Francis talked privately at Boulogne, they returned to Calais, where Anne – presented as though she was already queen – partnered Francis in a candlelit masque.[23]

At Francis's request, Clement issued the official docu-ments needed to make Cranmer Archbishop of Canterbury. But French lobbying in Rome suffered a major setback when, impetuously, Henry married Anne bigamously. After dancing with Francis, she was so confident a divorce was in sight that she finally agreed to sleep with Henry and the couple exchanged their wedding vows.[24] Now in her early thirties, and increasingly mindful of her promise to bear the king his coveted male heir, she had begun worrying about her own fertility. As it turned out, she knew by mid-February she was pregnant. Triumphantly, she teased all those around her by professing a sudden craving for apples.[25]

Henry sent Anne's brother George to give Francis the good news. But the French king fumed that the pregnancy made his task more difficult.[26] Cranmer's consecration as Archbishop of Canterbury, however, opened the door to the solution recommended by Foxe's dossier. With Anne three months pregnant, Henry decided to delay no longer. A bill prohibiting all appeals to Rome was introduced in

Parliament. Henry then declared that he recognized no superior on earth 'but only God', denouncing the pope as 'a violator of the rights of princes'.[27] He threatened, ominously, to 'open the eyes' of those of his fellow rulers who 'are not as learned as he is, and do not know that the real power of the pope is very small'.[28] Soon he could be found jotting down a note that papal jurisdiction had been exercised in England 'but only by negligence or usurpation as we take it and esteem'.[29]

In April 1533, Henry sent intermediaries to Katherine, tersely informing her for the very first time that he had married 'the other lady' more than two months before. The following month, Cranmer pronounced the verdicts for which the king had waited so long. Henry and Katherine, he proclaimed, had never been lawfully married, so Anne's marriage was valid.

Such was Henry's love for Anne that, briefly, he experimented with the idea of a joint coronation and began revising the coronation oath. Intriguingly, he seems to have envisaged a partnership in which, as in the medieval Byzantine Empire, consorts were 'joined to the purple by God's will' and possessed their own imperial seals: they could exercise real power and, occasionally, even become co-rulers with their husbands.

But with time pressing, Anne was crowned alone. The celebrations were the most dazzling of the reign and lasted over a fortnight.[30] In Henry's eyes, nothing was too good for his new queen. What shocked him was the sullen silence with which she was received in London. As her coronation procession slowly wended its way through the streets to

Westminster Abbey, many of the citizens refused to cry 'God save the Queen' or to doff their caps.[31]

In a final throw of the dice, Henry sent Thomas Howard, Duke of Norfolk, and George Boleyn back to Francis, who was on his way to greet the pope at Marseilles. Henry offered to finance a French invasion of Piedmont if Francis would join him in deposing and replacing Pope Clement. But Francis politely refused.[32]

Angry at what he saw as a sudden betrayal by his French ally and with Anne's baby due within weeks, Henry sent fresh envoys to give Clement an ultimatum. Denied access to the pope's apartments, one of the envoys forced his way in while Clement was eating breakfast, a discourtesy that upset Francis as much as the pope: Clement was his honoured guest.[33]

After that, Francis left Henry to stew, enraging him still further, since it was now clear to him that, if the perfidious French king was forced to choose between him and the pope, he would choose Clement. As the Duke of Norfolk confided to the French ambassador, Henry was 'so troubled in his brain about this matter that he does not trust anyone alive'.[34]

Anne's baby was born at Greenwich Palace between 3 and 4 o'clock in the afternoon of Sunday 7 September 1533. A daughter, rather than the son for whom Henry yearned, she was christened Elizabeth, after the king's mother.

A crescendo of opposition to Anne, meanwhile, had built up. A woman was imprisoned for saying Anne was a witch. Another called her 'a goggle-eyed whore' and prayed that she would never have another child by Henry.[35] Then a Canterbury nun, Elizabeth Barton, a woman who claimed to have divine visions and had previously had audiences with both Henry and Wolsey, began making political prophecies. Thomas More, who had sealed his fate in Henry's eyes by refusing to attend Anne's coronation, had met her, as had his good friend Bishop John Fisher of Rochester. More found Barton to be 'a right simple woman', although he had taken care to warn her how the Duke of Buckingham had been destroyed by the prophecies of a monk.

Barton, whose influence extended to the Franciscan friars and the London Carthusians, both of whom had been recipients of generous royal patronage in recent years, went on to denounce Henry's divorce and predicted that he would die of the plague, even claiming to have seen the place reserved for him in hell.[36] Furious that people he had once trusted and respected were turning against him, Henry ordered her to be locked up. And, at his insistence, Parliament declared her to be a traitor.[37]

On 23 March 1534, Pope Clement pronounced his long-awaited sentence on the divorce. It was a bombshell. Henry's first marriage to Katherine, he declared, was lawful. If the king refused to take her back, he would be excommunicated. And if he still remained obdurate, the sentence would be imposed by force.[38]

Clement's sentence made Henry more determined than ever. He believed that he was in the right, that God was on his side; and with the lawfulness of his second marriage on the line, no longer would he be prepared to respect other people's consciences. In any case, he had his reputation to defend as the heroic individual who would reverse the papal encroachments of the Middle Ages and restore the power of kings.

Three days later, Henry got Parliament to approve an Act of Succession that settled the crown on his heirs by Anne and that concluded with a clause requiring all males over fourteen to swear an oath affirming the 'whole effects and contents' of the act. This included that act's preamble, which declared that Anne's marriage was legally valid and that the pope had no right to meddle in the case. The penalty for refusing the oath was life imprisonment.[39]

Thomas More was Henry's first celebrity casualty. For refusing the oath, he and Fisher were sent to the Tower. Shortly afterwards, Elizabeth Barton and her backers – including several Franciscans and Carthusians – were dragged to the gallows. London's clergy and citizens were then required to take the oath en masse, after which the friaries at Canterbury, Greenwich and Richmond were purged and more cartloads of victims driven to the Tower.[40] Similar oath-takings followed all over England.

The swearing of the realm to the oath of succession was disrupted by a menacing insurrection across the Irish Sea. Suspecting Gerald Fitzgerald, Earl of Kildare, his chief governor in Ireland, of plotting against him, Henry had him arrested and sent to the Tower. But the move triggered a backlash for which Henry was entirely unprepared. The earl's son, Thomas, Lord Offaly, declared war: threatening to side with the pope and Charles V, he claimed that 10,000 Catholic troops were on their way to Ireland. In Dublin prominent Englishmen were murdered and the castle besieged.[41] Even when the revolt was suppressed, the Gaelic

Irish would continue a campaign of civil disobedience against Henry for years.[42]

In November 1534, Henry required Parliament to enshrine in an Act of Supremacy his title as 'Supreme Head on Earth of the Church' – this time without qualification. A draconian Treason Act swiftly followed. Now, it was high treason to traduce or threaten the royal family even by words, or to deny their titles (especially Henry's as Supreme Head).

The Treason Act did not pass unopposed: there was 'never', an eyewitness said, 'such a sticking at the passage of any Act'. A Commons committee considered it line by line, amending the bill to make sure it covered only words spoken 'maliciously' – seen as a vital reservation.[43]

The following spring, two Middlesex priests, both known to be strong supporters of the Carthusian order, railed against Henry from the pulpit, calling him 'a great tyrant . . . the cruellest, capital heretic puffed [up] with vainglory and pride' and saying of his private life that 'Thou shalt find it more foul and more stinking than a sow, wallowing and defiling herself in any filthy place'.[44] In a fury, Henry decided to make examples of them and of four Carthusian priors. He had the priests clapped in irons and the priors ordered to take a newly devised oath affirming Henry's title as Supreme Head of the Church, which they refused.

The priests pleaded guilty, but the priors tried a legal defence. They confessed they had denied the king's supremacy, but claimed they had not done so 'maliciously'. The judges ruled the distinction 'null and void'. When, despite the ruling, the jurors refused to convict, they were browbeaten until they brought in a guilty verdict.

Dragged across London from the Tower to Tyburn on hurdles, the priors were hanged from the gallows until almost unconscious, still wearing their religious dress. In a last-minute effort to so terrify them at the thought of what lay before them that they would change their minds and take the oath, Henry sent orders to the hangman to disembowel them one by one, in front of the others, while they were still alive. To silence their prayers, their genitals were cut off and stuffed into their mouths.[45]

This was Henry's justice. But his barbarity had a point – at least in his own mind – since his chief aim was not to kill the dissidents, but to coerce them into changing sides, reassuring him that he, and not the pope, was in the right.

Incredulous at the obstinacy and betrayal he perceived to be all around him, Henry rounded next on More and Fisher. Ordered to swear to the new oath of supremacy too, both refused, but neither would say why. Henry hesitated, conscious of the risk of making martyrs out of such eminent men. Then, in May 1535, the new pope, Paul III – he was elected by a sweeping majority after the death of Clement from a severe gastric disorder – made Fisher a cardinal.[46] Incensed at what he regarded as a deliberate provocation, the king, urged on by Anne, vowed to be avenged.

Fisher was easier to trap. Asked by Richard Rich, the Solicitor-General, for his off-the-record opinion, he made a forthright denial of Henry's claim to be the Supreme Head of the Church. At his trial that June, the judges instructed the jury to convict him as a matter of law, since he had admitted to speaking the words. 'The most part of the twelve men,' said an eyewitness, 'did this sore against their own conscience.' But individual consciences now counted for little: the only conscience that mattered was Henry's, so Fisher – sick from liver disease and barely able to walk – was carried on a mule to Tower Hill and beheaded.[47]

Thomas More proved harder to crack. That July, he was brought to trial without a watertight case against him. Rich had tried to trap him too, and when he failed, he committed perjury, testifying in court that More had denied the king's supremacy unambiguously – or so More's supporters have always maintained.

But before his sentence was handed down, More did at last speak his mind, defying Henry by invoking a legal ploy – his right to make a 'motion in arrest of judgement' – that allowed him to confront his accusers and declare on record that, in his opinion, the Act of Supremacy was legally invalid, because Parliament lacked sufficient authority to make such a law. More also deeply embarrassed the Duke of Norfolk by reminding him of the failure of his diplomacy with Francis.[48]

Henry's chief enforcer – the draughtsman of his parliamentary legislation since 1531, the man who browbeat the jurymen at the trial of the Carthusian priors, who several times interrogated Thomas More and who rigged the jury for his trial – was Wolsey's old fixer and solicitor, Thomas Cromwell.[49]

Cromwell, a Putney innkeeper's son and a self-made man, had wide experience of the world. In his twenties he was in Italy, fighting as a mercenary and working for the Frescobaldi merchant bank in Florence; while retraining as a lawyer in his early thirties, he made a number of visits to Rome. Henry had first encountered him after Wolsey's fall while searching for the disgraced minister's hidden assets. Instantly impressed, he took Cromwell into his service – but he would never link arms with him as he had with Wolsey, or call him his friend. Foreign ambassadors would never call him 'alter rex' or 'second king' as they had Wolsey. And whereas Wolsey, whenever he had wanted to see Henry, just walked in, Cromwell still had to make an appointment.

Within six weeks of making himself Supreme Head of the Church, Henry licensed Cromwell as his Vicar-General (or deputy) in Spiritual Affairs. His official task was to take a census of the wealth of the monasteries and list evidence of the laxity and corruption of the monks, but unofficially Cromwell helped Anne Boleyn to place evangelical preachers and chaplains in key positions, including bishoprics. He did this out of conviction. While studying law, he had made a living as a cloth exporter, in the process developing an intimate understanding of the commercial value of England's trading links with Charles V's territories and building lifelong relationships with several German Lutherans. His factor in Antwerp, Stephen Vaughan, was a passionate cheerleader for William Tyndale. For this, Cromwell had to walk a tightrope: Henry, whatever else he would do or come to believe, would never accept Luther's central theological doctrine of 'justification by faith alone'.*

Behind Henry's back, Cromwell arranged to import from

---

* Luther argued that grace, and therefore redemption, is solely at the will of a just, if merciful God. A justifying faith is imparted to

Cologne around 1,500 copies of the first complete English-language Bible, translated by Miles Coverdale, a lapsed Augustinian friar who had become a Lutheran and settled in Antwerp, not far from Tyndale. Cromwell then got one of his own contacts to reissue this edition from a shop in Southwark with a dedication to Henry, another move favoured by Anne.[50] Putting into circulation an English Bible without the king's explicit approval took some daring: at this stage Henry's own pet Bible project was a fresh edition of the old Latin Vulgate text, for which he wrote the preface and chose a special typeface.[51]

But Cromwell found Anne difficult to work with. In 1535, the pair were visibly at odds after Anne's brother George returned in unusual haste from Calais, where he had been discussing terms for a future marriage between the baby Elizabeth and the French king's third son. All was not well in Anglo-French relations and 'wrangling words' were exchanged at Calais and afterwards in the Privy Council.[52] Anne smouldered, but her position was vulnerable. Four months after Elizabeth's birth, she had miscarried, and it took over a year for her to conceive again. Henry, meanwhile, was flirting with another woman.[53] He quickly dropped his new amour – but that was only because he had transferred his affections to Mary Shelton, Anne's cousin.[54]

By October 1535, Anne was pregnant again: she and Henry were said to be 'very merry' and debating points of religion at mealtimes.[55] But a dark cloud was on the

---

God's elect, i.e. those who will be saved, that has nothing to do with their own earthly actions or those of the pope and clergy.

horizon. A month earlier, the royal couple had stayed for five days with Sir John Seymour and his wife at Wolf Hall in Wiltshire and Henry had met Jane, one of Sir John's daughters. Aged twenty-six, she was fashionably pale, of middling height and not a noted beauty – but she caught the king's eye.[56]

When Katherine died on 7 January 1536, Henry and Anne both dressed in yellow satin, avoiding black, the conventional colour of mourning, to flaunt their glee. The stage, it seemed, was set for Anne's triumph.[57] But three weeks later, calamity struck: she miscarried a male foetus, said to be about three and a half months old.[58]

Anne blamed the disaster on a horrific shock she had received five days earlier. While jousting at Greenwich, Henry had been unseated by an opponent, hitting the ground while fully armed, his horse falling on top of him. This was his third major sporting accident. In the lists twelve years previously, he had been struck in the face by the Duke of Suffolk's lance after he forgot to lower his visor. The following year, while out hawking, he had attempted to vault a stream with a pole: the pole broke and he fell headfirst into the mud.[59] But this latest incident was more serious. After lying unconscious for almost two hours, Henry managed to stumble to his feet and declare that he 'had no hurt'. All the same, it would not be long before he would admit to trouble with an ulcer on his left leg, possibly the result of varicose veins, but more likely caused by chronic osteomyelitis, a septic infection of the bone.[60]

Henry, however, never had time for anyone's excuses but his own. When, that same January, the news of Anne's miscarriage was brought to him, his response was simply, 'I see that God will not give me male children,' after which he walked away.[61] Soon he was sending presents to Jane Seymour. He was also voicing his doubts about Anne, telling those around him that he had married her while 'seduced by witchcraft'.[62]

On 2 April, Anne clashed publicly with Cromwell for encouraging Henry to believe that he should suppress the smaller abbeys in order to bolster his finances. She had no quarrel with the suppression as such, but wanted the money put towards education and poor relief instead. And to ram home her point, she had one of her chaplains, John Skip, preach a sermon at Whitehall with her husband present. In a thinly veiled allusion, Skip denounced Cromwell as Haman, who in the Old Testament Book of Esther had deceived King Ahasuerus into ordering a massacre of his Jewish subjects. Skip even dared to swipe at the king's interest in Jane Seymour, many of whose relatives and allies were religious conservatives. As Jane rose in the king's favour, rivalry between her supporters and Anne's was inevitable, showing that Henry was fast losing control of his Court.[63]

Anne's tongue was her undoing. On the 29th of that month, she quarrelled with Sir Henry Norris, the chief gentleman of the king's Privy Chamber. Loose talk got out of hand when she teased him over his own sexual relationship with her cousin Mary Shelton. Why had he not married her? When Norris replied that he 'would tarry a time', Anne rashly retorted, 'You look for dead men's shoes, for if ought should come to the king but good, you would look to have me.'[64]

Their conversation was overheard and the backstairs whisperers went into overdrive. That evening or the next day, Henry and Anne had a furious row. The king claimed that Norris had cuckolded him. Anne loudly protested her innocence, causing Henry to pause, but the seeds of doubt were sown.

As the king tossed and turned in his bed overnight, his mind swung violently against Anne. After the May Day jousts at Greenwich, he rose abruptly from his seat and, as he rode back to London, questioned Norris intently. He had decided to ditch Anne, whose indictment – drafted by Cromwell – accused her of plotting to corrupt the allegiance of Norris and three other alleged lovers, in order that one of them would kill Henry and marry her, an allegation Cromwell spiced up with a shocking charge of incest with her brother George.[65]

Very likely it was Henry's emotional revulsion at the mutterings of incest – fed to him on the eve of the May Day jousts – that did most to turn his long infatuation with Anne into a sudden murderous loathing. Despite their often stormy relationship, she was the love of his life. But the suggestion of incest – so reminiscent of the revulsion he had come to feel for Katherine – sent him over the edge. Rarely did he destroy people on the spur of the moment; he would tend to brood first for days or even weeks. In Anne's case, however, a torrent of jealousy, moral abhorrence and vengeful spite drove him uncontrollably forward. He believed that the scales had fallen from his eyes.

Norris and his fellow courtiers were tried and condemned on the 12th of May, Anne and her brother George on the

15th.[66] George caused a sensation by defying the court's orders and reading out a paper submitted in evidence that said his sister had once told his wife Jane in an unguarded moment that Henry suffered from erectile dysfunction.[67]

On the 17th, the alleged partners in Anne's sexual crimes, including George, were beheaded. On the same day, Cranmer pronounced Henry's second marriage invalid. Two days later, Anne was executed by a single blow of a sword – her head fell to the ground with her lips and eyes still moving.

Within a fortnight, Henry exchanged his marriage vows with Jane Seymour in the queen's oratory at Whitehall.[68] Next, Parliament was recalled to debate the Second Act of Succession, which nullified the claims arising from Henry's earlier marriages and declared both his daughters illegitimate. Now, only Jane's offspring would be able to claim the throne.[69]

In Rome, Pope Paul rejoiced that Henry was free of a woman Katherine of Aragon's supporters had always called 'the concubine'. He put out an olive branch, proposing reconciliation and inviting Henry to send delegates to a future General Council of the Church at Mantua. Trapped between the warring powers in Italy, the new pope sought to tempt Henry to reclaim the role of arbiter of international disputes he had briefly played after the Treaty of Universal Peace in 1518.[70]

But first, declared Pope Paul, Henry had to reverse the break with Rome and receive absolution. It was a fresh turning point, and the consequences would be as profound as anything that had gone before.

4
Arbiter of Christendom

Safely married to Jane Seymour and with Pope Clement dead, Henry had the perfect opportunity to reverse his break with Rome. Pope Paul had offered reconciliation. Charles V, under attack from Lutheranism in Germany and the Ottoman Turks in the Mediterranean, was keen to restore his old amity now that both Katherine of Aragon and Anne Boleyn were dead. Jane's supporters were conservative – unlike Anne, she was certainly no patron of evangelical reformers.

Many of Henry's subjects believed that, free of Anne, he would revert to his old self and repudiate the Royal Supremacy. They could not have been more wrong. Hardened by what he considered to be the mendacity of those who opposed him, he refused to admit any mistakes, signalling his intransigence in the most visceral of ways by demanding that Mary, his daughter with Katherine of Aragon, subscribe to the Act of Supremacy and acknowledge that her parents' marriage had been 'incestuous and unlawful'. As with her mother before her, Henry spoke to Mary through intermediaries. Arriving on one occasion, they threatened her, saying that 'If she was their daughter, they would beat her and knock her head so violently against the wall that they would make it as soft as baked apples'.[1] Cromwell brought such pressure to bear on Mary to sign that, finally, she could endure the ordeal no longer and obeyed.[2]

Henry then lashed out at other members of his family, especially those with Yorkist lineage. He began with Reginald Pole, whom he had restored to favour at the beginning of his reign and for whose studies at Oxford and Padua he had largely paid. Reginald had quarrelled with Henry in 1532 over the king's attacks on the Church, which he regarded as unlawful, and gone into exile in Italy. Still willing then to respect other people's consciences, Henry had left him alone for three more years before declaring that Pole had betrayed him. In 1535, he insisted that Pole set forth in confidence his opinions of both the king's divorce and break with Rome, and Pole reluctantly offered to comply. A year later, he sent Henry what can only be described as a vitriolic broadside.[3]

Henry was incensed. With his infinite capacity for vengeful disenchantment when disappointed by those he regarded as close to him, he thirsted for revenge. Undeterred by Pole's attack, he swiftly pushed ahead with his plans to suppress the smaller abbeys. To his amazement, his new wife, Jane – hitherto all obedience – dared to criticize him.

Matters came to a head in October 1536, when, in protest at the annihilation of the abbeys, first Lincolnshire and then the whole of Yorkshire and the north erupted in mass insurrections. The largest of these rebellions, called the Pilgrimage of Grace, was the biggest threat faced by either Henry or his father, so dangerous because nobles (mainly lesser nobility), gentry, clergy and some 40,000 commoners joined forces in a bid to force the king to dismiss Cromwell and Cranmer, and then summon a Parliament at which he would reverse all his policies.[4] Jane threw herself on her knees and implored Henry to restore the abbeys, but he told her to get up and stop interfering. 'Remember,' he snapped, 'that the last queen died in consequence of meddling too much.'[5]

Henry defeated the rebels as much through guile as by force. Negotiations between the Duke of Norfolk and the rebel leadership led first to a truce and then a pardon.[6] But the king had no intention of honouring the peace, treating the rebels to a hefty dose of psychological warfare by inviting their captain, Robert Aske, to Greenwich to share in his Christmas festivities.[7] Inevitably the visit aroused the suspicions of Aske's fellow rebels, leading to a split. Further revolts early in the New Year then enabled Henry to divide and rule, besides claiming that the rebels' fresh treasons had broken the truce.[8]

Henry ordered the reprisals to be 'without pity or respect'. 'It shall,' he proclaimed, 'be much better that these traitors should perish' so that 'the terror of this execution' should forever be remembered.[9] One of his more astonishing moves after suppressing the revolts was to rewrite the Sixth Commandment, to make it clear that rulers could kill and coerce their subjects without recourse to the 'just order of their laws'. The change did not survive Cranmer's scrutiny – it was quickly reversed – but little could better illustrate the direction in which Henry's thoughts were turning.[10]

The insurrections had been defeated, but in Henry's own mind the crisis was far from over. When, in December 1536, the pope made Reginald Pole a cardinal with instructions to raise funds to bankroll the rebels, the king turned on his fugitive kinsman with renewed venom.[11] Now out to silence him for good, he sent assassins across the Channel to kidnap or kill him. He also offered a bounty to anyone who would bring him Pole, dead or alive.[12]

Henry's intransigence, however, was not solely a result of his pride, ambition or even the desire for a male heir. Underpinning his stance was the beginning of a further seismic shift in his opinions, this time in the direction of the religious reformers. An early signal of this was an embassy he sent in late 1535 to Wittenberg, the very heart of Lutheranism. The mission aimed at reaching an accord with the federation of German Protestant princes and cities known as the Schmalkaldic League, which had been formed to shield the Lutheran territories from the reprisals of the emperor and pope.[13]

As Henry explained his position to the French king, Francis I, the General Council of the Church proposed by Pope Paul could be acceptable to him if correctly convened – he meant by secular rulers rather than the pope – and if held in a safe and neutral place.[14] If those conditions were met, he would feel morally obliged to attend. Hence it would be prudent for him to reach a consensus with the members of the League on the key issues they might each be called upon to defend.[15]

Henry had a gleam in his eye. If the Council met in the manner and form that he prescribed, he might himself preside over it, and in so doing, he might make himself – rather than the pope – the arbiter of Christendom.

With this end in view, he set about redefining the doctrines of his 'own' Church of England along lines that he
hoped could bridge the wider Reformation divide.[16] Hardly
surprisingly, the Germans saw it differently. If he wanted to
ally himself with their League, he must instead accept their
own manifesto of religious faith, the Confession of Augs-
burg, and with it Luther's central doctrine of 'justification
by faith alone'. Since Henry refused, still believing this
aspect of Luther's theology to be heretical, his diplomacy
was halted in its tracks.

Cromwell, however, had different ideas. He used the dis-
cussion paper Foxe brought back from Germany as a
template for his own 'Ten Articles . . . to establish Christian
quietness and unity', enforced in August 1536 by royal
injunctions.[17] Cromwell's Articles set forth his own more
radical religious agenda. But to Henry, they were a step too
far towards Lutheranism. The following year he ordered
Cromwell to replace them with a more far-reaching confes-
sional statement known as *The Institution of a Christian
Man*.[18] Explaining the king's rationale to Cranmer and the
bishops, Cromwell said that Henry sought to dispel 'certain
controversies which at this time be moved concerning the
Christian religion and faith, not only in this realm, but also
in all nations through the world'. Henry in future wanted
doctrines to be based purely on the 'Word of God', purged
of any superfluous 'glosses or papistical laws', or indeed
anything else 'not contained in the Scripture'.[19]

Cromwell's announcement reflected a dramatic change
to Henry's underlying belief system as compared to the
views he had held when he had written his book against

Luther in 1521. Whereas before, Henry had always maintained that he was a 'true Catholic' and scourge of the reformers, now for the first time he allowed himself to be quoted in print using the vocabulary of a spiritual conversion. 'We princes,' he suddenly proclaimed in an official protestation composed most likely over the winter of 1537–8, 'wrote ourselves to be inferiors to popes: as long as we thought so, we obeyed them as our superiors. Now, we write not as we did.' And to prove his point, he added, 'Christ said, "I am the way, truth and life." He never said, "I am the custom."' He then went on to explain that, whereas Rome's theology was rooted in dark inventions and ancient superstitions, his own was based purely on Scripture – as indeed was Luther's own.[20]

From this point onwards, Henry was the author of his own distinctive brand of reformed theology. At its heart was the 'Word of God' as set forth in the Bible: this Henry had come to regard as equivalent to a 'super-sacrament'. It was the cornerstone on which all the other sacraments were built, and upon which they depended. His spiritual quest did not end with *The Institution of a Christian Man*, which he replaced in 1543 with the more comprehensive, if less radical, *Necessary Doctrine and Erudition for Any Christian Man*.[21] Along the way – and to the Lutherans' deep dismay – he asked Parliament in 1539 to pass an Act of Six Articles, trying to square a religious circle by once more enforcing what at first sight seemed to be a more traditional Catholic interpretation of the seven sacraments of the Church.

Henry's reversion in his later years to a more Catholic

1. The frontispiece of the presentation copy of Henry's *Assertio Septem Sacramentorum*, sent to Leo X in 1521 and showing Henry kneeling for a papal blessing

2. A painted terracotta bust by Guido Mazzoni, said to be of Henry as a seven-year-old boy (c.1498)

3. Henry jousting before Katherine of Aragon in 1511

4. Henry riding in procession at the Field of Cloth of Gold with Wolsey beside him on a mule, 1520. Wolsey designed for Henry the magnificent temporary palace seen in the foreground on the right.

5. A detail from one of the treaty documents recording the terms ratified between Henry and Francis I at Amiens in 1527. Although the image shows a (fictitious) meeting between Francis (centre left) and Henry (centre right), it was Wolsey who confirmed the treaty with the French king.

6. The classic image of Henry by Hans Holbein the Younger, who grasped to perfection the psyche of a king who could declare with pride: 'By God, I trust no one but myself'

7. Thomas Cromwell by Hans Holbein the Younger. The artist deliberately typecast Cromwell as a workaholic man of affairs.

8. The hanging and disembowelling of the Carthusian priors in
1535 for denying Henry's new title of Supreme Head of the Church.
An artist's impression, engraved in Rome.

Dominus illuminatio mea & sa-
lus mea: quem timebo:
Dominus protector vitæ meæ a quo

9. David and Goliath, showing Henry as David, from the king's
psalter, written and illuminated by Jean Mallard, 1540

10. Henry as he approached age fifty-five. A posthumous image by Cornelis Metsys, engraved at Antwerp in *c*.1548.

reading of the sacraments, however, was more apparent than real. His Six Articles, for all the notoriety they attracted among the Protestants, continued to reflect the king's heightened emphasis on Scripture as the test by which the Church and its doctrines should be judged.[22] Whereas Catholics saw the act of consecration at the Mass as a miracle performed by the mediation of the clergy, the Six Articles claimed that it was achieved only 'by the strength and efficacy of Christ's mighty Word' (the words of consecration being merely *spoken* by the priest).[23]

Henry's theology ended up as a somewhat idiosyncratic mix, leaving him looking very much like a beached whale, stranded on the sandbanks between Rome and Wittenberg. His spiritual journey would be hesitant at best, but if instinctively he recoiled from the most central of Luther's doctrines, neither would he remain an orthodox Catholic.[24]

By the summer of 1537, Jane Seymour was pregnant and Henry said he dared not leave her side. With the king so distracted, Cromwell gently coaxed him into the important step of licensing the so-called 'Matthew Bible' – a version of Tyndale's text made by his assistant John Rogers, using the pseudonym Thomas Matthew so as to distance the project from Tyndale.[25] Cranmer rejoiced at the news, telling Henry, 'You have showed me more pleasure herein than if you had given me £1,000.'[26] The new licence also applied to Coverdale's translation, but for Cromwell it was not yet enough. Now, his ambition was to get a vernacular Bible into all 8,500 parish churches in England.

On 12 October, Jane was delivered of a healthy boy,

christened Edward. She seemed to be recovering well following an excruciating labour, but died twelve days later after bleeding heavily.[27] Henry doted on his son. He also professed himself grief-stricken for Jane – even if, within a fortnight of her funeral, he was putting out feelers for a new wife.[28]

Despite having at last fathered a legitimate male heir, after more than a quarter-century of trying, Henry still felt disturbingly vulnerable. Just a month after Edward's birth, Francis I and Charles V ended yet another round of bitter Franco-Habsburg warfare with a truce, later extended for ten years in a deal masterminded by Pope Paul.[29] This left Henry further away than ever from his goal of becoming the arbiter of Christendom as part of his quest for fame. In an attempt to regain lost ground, he reopened talks with the Schmalkaldic League.[30]

In May 1538, as a second German delegation arrived in England, Cromwell saw his opportunity, pressing ahead with measures that would impress the League while advancing his own agenda.[31] With Henry having now denounced veneration of relics and images as idolatry pure and simple – despite his own pilgrimages and offerings to saints as a younger man – the Vicar-General's men purged shrines and cults of saints with unconcealed zest, to the delight of the king's German guests.[32] Most spectacularly, the shrine of Thomas Becket at Canterbury, one of the richest in Europe and at which Henry had himself once knelt in prayer with Charles V, was flattened and despoiled and the saint's bones scattered to the wind.[33]

Already Henry had ordered the destruction of the

larger abbeys, declaring them to be inveterate bastions of 'popery'. Those monks who co-operated were generously pensioned off. Those who resisted – among them the Abbots of Colchester, Reading and Glastonbury – were bound in chains, tried for treason and hanged. Their beautiful cloisters and abbey-churches, apart from a number Henry kept and turned into cathedrals, were dismantled – in some cases using explosives in a concerted effort to wipe their memory from the face of the earth. Precious metals, art treasures, libraries and building materials were systematically plundered. Henry's first official act as a young prince had been to witness a charter to the monks of Glastonbury, granting them the right to hold annual fairs. Now, he flattened their abbey, looted their treasure and displayed the abbot's severed head above its gateway on a pole.[34]

But negotiations with the League faltered again when Henry declined to make concessions on such topics as communion in both the bread and the wine, private Masses and clerical celibacy.[35] And as the Germans gloomily made their way home from England, another theological stumbling block began to loom.

The Lutherans had always been as flatly opposed as Henry to the purely symbolic view of the Eucharist that a number of the more advanced Swiss reformers had been developing in Zurich. Labelled as 'sacramentarianism' by its opponents, this doctrine (in which Christ was said to be only 'figuratively present' in the sacrament) was regarded by Henry as loathsome. Now, he began to receive information of a sacramentarian network operating in England. Cranmer's inquiries uncovered a flagrant suspect; to make it even more embarrassing for Henry, the man, John Lambert, when accused, appealed to the king to be his judge and asked for the opportunity to meet his accusers in open debate.[36] Henry decided to make an example of him. Putting on 'priestly' garments, the king – flanked by Cromwell and the bishops – convened Lambert's heresy trial in the White Hall at Westminster, near to St Stephen's Chapel. The proceedings ended after five hours with the accused being dragged away to be roasted alive at Smithfield.[37]

By then, Henry's attempts to assassinate or kidnap Reginald Pole had failed miserably, so – urged on by Cromwell – he wreaked vengeance on his kinsman's relatives instead. The most exalted of them, Henry Courtenay, whom Henry had raised to the peerage as Marquis of Exeter and with whom he had once enjoyed a snowball fight, was sent to the Tower alongside Reginald's brothers, Henry and Geoffrey. After humbly submitting himself to the king and admitting that he had burned incriminating letters from Reginald, Geoffrey was pardoned. Courtenay and Henry Pole, fiercely interrogated and then tried and convicted on Geoffrey's evidence, were at once beheaded.[38]

Not even Reginald's sixty-six-year-old mother, Margaret, Countess of Salisbury, would escape the cull. She denied everything and in reluctant admiration her inquisitors confessed: 'We suppose that there hath not been seen or heard of a woman so earnest in her constancy and so manlike in continuance.' Either her sons had not made her privy to their intentions, 'or else she is the most arrant traitress that ever lived'. Attainted for treason by Parliament, she was sent to the Tower. There, Henry kept her on tenterhooks (if in some style) for two more years before sending her to the scaffold.[39]

Pope Paul could wait no longer. On 17 December 1538, he proclaimed a decree excommunicating Henry, declaring him an outcast from the Church.[40] Without further delay, Reginald Pole published the broadside he had earlier sent in confidence to the king, denouncing Henry as spiritually and mentally diseased and as a murderous tyrant worse than Nero or Richard III. For his demonic usurpation of the pope's lawful powers and other acts of sacrilege, Pole said, Henry was destined to burn in hell. Pole then hurried to Toledo in an effort to persuade Charles V to invade England.

In response, Henry put England on full military alert. He personally inspected the fortifications at Dover, and gave orders to refit and greatly enlarge the royal navy, muster troops and embark on a massive operation to reconstruct the coastal defences. At Berwick on the frontier with Scotland, the fortifications were rebuilt, and along the whole of the south coast from the Thames to Milford Haven a chain of new fortresses was constructed. This was the largest military building programme between the Norman Conquest and the Napoleonic Wars. To pay for it, Henry was forced to tax his subjects as never before and begin selling the abbey lands on an epic scale.[41]

Taking a subtler approach to the threat, Cromwell proposed that Henry make a marriage alliance with the Schmalkaldic League. Henry's search for a new wife had so far been unsuccessful. The first serious candidate to rule herself out was Christina – sixteen-year-old daughter of the deposed Christian II of Denmark and niece of Charles V – who had married the Duke of Milan and, since his death three years before, was now a widow. The proposal had been well received by Charles, less so by Christina – perhaps unsurprisingly, given Henry's way with wives. In any case, Henry's conditions were so unreasonable that the negotiations fell apart.[42]

Henry had then turned to France, proposing that a beauty parade of seven or eight potential brides be arranged for him at Calais. When the outraged French ambassador objected, suggesting instead that Henry send someone to interview them privately, the king retorted, 'By God, I trust no one but myself.' The ambassador's response was acid: 'Would you not, Sir, therefore rather mount them, one after the other, and afterwards keep for yourself the one you found the most alluring? Would not the Knights of the Round Table have treated their women like that?' At this, even Henry had to blush.[43]

Cromwell's preferred candidate was Anne, daughter of Duke John III of Cleves. She had once been contracted to marry the Duke of Lorraine's son, a difficulty that Cromwell rashly believed could be swiftly fixed.[44] This was not quite a perfect match – Cleves was not yet a formal member of the Schmalkaldic League, although it was preparing to join. From Henry's viewpoint, the idea had the greater merit in that Duke John and his son and heir, William, stood on the middle ground between Rome and Wittenberg in theology – ground that he was of course keen to occupy himself.[45]

The bonus was that Anne of Cleves was said to be unusually beautiful. Henry had ordered checks on her appearance: all the reports were favourable. Keen to see for himself, Henry sent the artist Hans Holbein the Younger across the Channel to paint her portrait as he had done before with Christina of Milan. The results were inviting: Henry believed he saw a perfectly poised young woman, with pale skin, soft eyes, a slightly wide nose and a delicate mouth. It was true that she spoke only German and was said to be no musician, but he thought such drawbacks could be remedied.

After a treaty was concluded, Anne set out for England, by which time Cromwell had secured Henry's approval for a new 'Great Bible', a much improved revision of the earlier translations and a milestone in English printing history. Over the next two years, 9,000 copies were sold at a subsidized price so that every parish church could purchase one, enabling Cromwell to fulfil his lifelong ambition to put the Scripture in the hands of the ordinary people.

Arriving in winter after a brief stay in Calais, Anne of Cleves was taken to Greenwich Palace, where the wedding took place on 6 January 1540. But from the moment Henry saw his intended bride, he disliked her. At Rochester on New Year's Day, he had rushed to meet her, laden with gifts, but did not give them to her. Only under protest – as he cautioned Cromwell – was he prepared to 'put his neck in the yoke'.[46]

The wedding night was a disaster. When Henry (as he complained next day) examined Anne's 'belly and breasts', he decided that 'she was no maid'.[47] Over the ensuing months, he made a number of further fumbling attempts at consummation, but to no avail. And with Cromwell fatally weakened by a debacle in which he had allowed his religious passions to overrule his head, his court enemies moved in for the kill. Now, the man whom Henry had made his Vicar-General in Spiritual Affairs was roundly denounced as a heretic for allegedly protecting a secret cell of sacramentarians at Calais.[48] In the circumstances, the charge was inherently plausible, just as, in the king's eyes, Cromwell's dealings over the Cleves marriage had been treasonable.[49] Prepared to listen to Cromwell's enemies as he never had before, Henry gave the orders for his chief minister to be arrested and thrown into the Tower.

Cromwell fought like a tiger to save himself. But when his house was searched, incriminating papers were found. Some related to a clandestine contact with the Swiss reformers;[50] others proved to Henry's satisfaction that Cromwell had lied to him over precisely when proof had been obtained that Anne's earlier marriage contract to the Duke of Lorraine's son had been annulled.[51]

Like Wolsey before him, Cromwell had outlived his usefulness to Henry. Another victim of the king's deadly impatience in the face of knotty problems, he was executed on 28 July 1540, after providing from the Tower the evidence Henry needed to have his marriage to Anne of Cleves annulled on the grounds of non-consummation.[52]

The king's eye had already lighted on Katherine Howard, whom he visited secretly at her grandmother's house at Lambeth across the Thames from Whitehall while still married to Anne of Cleves. The niece of Thomas Howard, Duke of Norfolk, and barely out of her teens, Katherine became Henry's fifth wife and for the next fifteen months his great passion – he called her his 'jewel' – until she was denounced to Cranmer for her reckless indiscretions with an old flame.[53]

By the time Katherine was beheaded at the Tower, on Monday 13 February 1542, international affairs had started to look rosier for Henry. Once more he began to look eagerly to the continent, ever anxious to rediscover the fame and recognition he had previously enjoyed at the time of the Treaty of Universal Peace of 1518 and the Field of Cloth of Gold two years later. No longer would he seek to bridge the Reformation divide: instead he would once more offer his services to Francis I and Charles V as the arbiter of international disputes.

The omens were favourable in that Pope Paul's attempts to convene a General Council to rebuild the unity of the Catholic Church had fatally stalled and Pole's efforts to persuade the Catholic powers to invade England met a similar fate. When in June 1541 the ten-year truce between Francis and Charles masterminded by the pope collapsed in acrimony, Henry felt that his moment had come.[54] He reproached Francis for his great folly in trusting the pope.[55] And he dropped the broadest of hints: 'if our wit, power, authority or friendship might do anything . . . we would yet be glad to employ it to both your commodities and the benefit and quiet of Christendom'.[56]

But Francis allied himself with the pope, in addition to Venice, some of the Lutheran princes and (scandalously, given their infidel status) the Ottoman Turks, ignoring Henry, who instead made overtures to Charles.[57] First, however, Henry turned towards Scotland. His nephew James V promised to meet him at York, and then stood him up. The insult exasperated Henry, who some years before had failed to bully James into breaking with Rome. For the first time in writing to a fellow monarch, he let his temper rip, provoking James into spiting Henry by marrying a French bride – and, when she died, another.[58] In response, Henry reiterated his claim to be Scotland's feudal overlord. Indignant at his nephew's defiant attitude, he meant to detach the Scots from Francis's clutches for ever, whatever the cost.[59]

In August 1542, Henry sent the Duke of Norfolk to raid the Scottish border. At first little was achieved. Then a Scottish army crossed into England, only to be trapped between a peat bog known as Solway Moss and the swirling waters of the River Esk. Hundreds of men and horses were drowned and dozens of nobles captured. On top of this, within a month the Scottish king died from what was believed to be either dysentery or cholera. Now, Scotland seemed to be at Henry's mercy, the country's fortunes tied to those of James's infant daughter Mary – later, Mary, Queen of Scots – born six days before James died.[60]

Henry had plans for Mary, his great-niece. He would bring her up in England and marry her to Prince Edward, thereby engineering a dynastic union of England and Scotland. Summoning his most important Scottish prisoners south, he worked on them psychologically, first throwing them into the Tower to soften them up, before bringing them to Court, dressing them in the finest black damask gowns and entertaining them royally over Christmas.[61] Before ransoming them and sending them home, Henry forced them to sign articles committing the Scots to agree to his plans.[62] When the Scottish Parliament then refused his terms, he threatened to 'exterminate' the Scots 'to the third and fourth generation'.[63]

In May 1544, the Earl of Hertford – Jane Seymour's brother and Henry's top general – sailed up the Firth of Forth to put the king's threat into action. His orders were to burn and sack Edinburgh and the countryside of Fife, 'putting man, woman and child to fire and sword'. Hertford reported to Henry that he had made 'a jolly fire and smoke upon the town' and left Edinburgh and the royal palace of Holyrood 'in manner wholly burnt and desolate'.[64]

Francis, meanwhile, had declared war on Charles and invaded imperial territory.[65] Henry's response was to make a league with Charles, ratified near Barcelona in May 1543 and published in June. Reworking the plan Charles and Wolsey had once devised for the Great Enterprise, the allies agreed to launch a combined invasion of France as soon as Hertford had finished in Scotland. Charles was to march into France from the east, Henry from the north, and their armies were to converge on Paris. The difference was that Henry would personally take command.[66]

This last decision greatly troubled his councillors. Now fifty-two, Henry was becoming vastly obese. After his terrible jousting accident in 1536, his sporting days were largely over. He never jousted again and his ability to hunt became increasingly restricted. In other words, he no longer took the daily exercise he had always been used to, despite continuing to eat voraciously. His health and mobility had consequently plummeted.[67]

According to measurements taken for his most recent suit of armour, his chest circumference had ballooned to 57 inches and his waistline to 54.[68] The ulcer on his left leg – now complemented by one on his right – left him barely able to stand, often confined to bed for days at a time.[69] But because Charles insisted on leading his own armies, Henry felt he had to do the same – not to do so would risk losing face.

Yet Henry had grown so irascible, his moods so unpredictable, that no one dared tell him of the risks associated with such a venture.[70] Certainly nobody dared mention his sore legs for fear of ending up in the Tower.

A month after the Anglo-imperial league was ratified, Henry took Katherine Parr, the thirty-one-year-old widow of John Neville, Lord Latimer, as his sixth and last queen.[71] Vivacious and sensuous, she was of middling height, with auburn hair and grey eyes and a passion for jewels, clothes and shoes. Henry called her 'sweetheart' and let her sit on his lap. He was in love with her when they married. A verse message he scribbled to her reads: 'Remember this writer / when you do pray / for he is yours / none can say nay.'[72] All the same, his affection was not so great that she could presume to change the ladies in her bedchamber without seeking his permission.[73]

In July 1544, Henry set out for Calais with his army, embarking on a ship trimmed with sails of cloth of gold. On arrival, he led an assault on the town and port of Bou-logne.[74] That deviated sharply from his agreement with Charles: Henry did this because he did not fully trust his ally, remembering how the emperor had double-crossed him after the Battle of Pavia. If that were not enough, Henry lectured Charles on strategy and the dangers of advancing into the heart of France. 'It would be far better,' he said, 'to lay siege to two or three towns on the road to Paris, than to go to the capital and burn it down.'[75]

After Henry laid a mine under the castle and exploded it, Boulogne surrendered and he entered the town in tri-umph.[76] But his strident efforts to dictate the course of the war so irritated Charles that the emperor made a separate peace with Francis, running rings round Henry, whom he deliberately locked into the war by exploiting a clause in their league that required his consent to any of Henry's own peace proposals.[77]

Oblivious to the consequences of his arrogance, Henry returned home, handing over command to the Duke of Norfolk and then to the latter's son, the dashing young Henry Howard, Earl of Surrey. To secure Boulogne, how-ever, they were forced to dig in. Thereafter, Henry found himself fighting on two fronts: Francis had sent naval and military reinforcements to Scotland and so the Earl of Hert-ford was despatched to devastate the Scottish Lowlands once more.[78]

But Henry's greatest military humiliations were still to come. In February 1545, the Scots lured an English army into a trap at Ancrum Moor near Jedburgh, killing 800 sol-diers and capturing 1,000. Then, that spring, Francis began to make ready his main fleet. In July, over 120 French ships boldly entered the Solent, eager to disrupt Henry's supply lines to Boulogne and to attack the English fleet in its own anchorage. Warned of their approach while dining with his captains on his flagship, the *Henry Grace à Dieu*, Henry ordered his fleet to put to sea and was hastily rowed to land. Before his very eyes, his favourite warship, the *Mary Rose*, keeled over in a strong gust of wind while going about to assist the *Henry Grace à Dieu*, which was being challenged by the more mobile French galleys. The ship sank with the loss of 500 men. The gun ports had, it seemed, been left open ready to fire a broadside: they were only about 4 feet above the waterline, and when the ship unexpectedly turned, the sea flooded in.[79]

The war did not end before Henry tried one last throw of the dice. In a brazen attempt to outflank Charles and recruit trained mercenaries to help defend Boulogne, he opened up a final round of negotiations for what he described as a 'League Christian' with the Lutheran princes, themselves still at loggerheads with the emperor.[80]

A German delegation visited England in the spring of 1546, but saw straight through Henry's schemes, which had little or nothing to do with the defence of their faith and everything to do with Henry's desire to retain his recent gains in northern France.

After the best part of two years, Henry and Francis at last came to terms, and, in June 1546, Henry's army retreated back across the Channel.

Henry gained temporary control of Boulogne – the terms of the new treaty stipulated that he had to sell it back to

Francis within eight years – and French suspension of military aid to Scotland. But the costs of his French adventure had been ruinous. To pay for it, he had to sell all but a handful of the remainder of the abbey lands that Cromwell had wanted him to keep, to levy annual taxes and repeatedly debase the coinage, with disastrous economic effects.

Having set out to achieve his long-coveted role as arbiter of international disputes, Henry had ended up overreaching himself. Far from winning fame and recognition, he had become isolated, even marginalized, on the European stage. To remain in the game, he had privately to swallow his pride and pretend that, whatever might be their temporary misunderstandings, he and Charles were still the best of friends.[81]

By the time Pope Paul did finally succeed in convening a General Council of the Church in 1545, Henry had become an irrelevance.[82] Even within the British Isles, the dynastic union he had sought to bring about was fatally compromised. If that was not enough, endemic factionalism on a scale never seen before was about to take root at Court and split it down the middle.

5
A Second Solomon

Like King Solomon, the most famous of the Old Testament patriarchs, who was said to have sat in majesty on an ivory throne and who completed the building of the First Temple in Jerusalem, Henry regarded magnificence as a political weapon. His father was the earliest English ruler to employ Italian sculptors on royal building projects, such as his dynastic mausoleum in the Lady Chapel of Westminster Abbey, but Henry was the first to drag the monarchy kicking and screaming into the mainstream of the European Renaissance.

He dressed to impress, spending up to £4,000 a year on clothes at a time when his personal tailor, John Malt, earned as little as 12 pence a day (in old, pre-decimal currency). Apart from robes of state, his wardrobe contained 79 thickly bejewelled gowns, many with collars of lynx, sable or squirrel fur, 86 coats and 134 doublets made from 29 types of fabric, including 25 of velvet, 23 of 'tilsent' (a prohibitively expensive silk cloth interwoven with flat gold or silver metallic strips) and 17 of satin. Sometimes he wore contrasting colours, at other times the same, as on May Day 1510 when he burst into Katherine of Aragon's bedchamber, dressed all in green like Robin Hood and clutching a bow and arrow, or the day the news of Katherine of Aragon's death broke, when he and Anne Boleyn put on matching yellow satin.[1]

A compulsive purchaser of accessories, he got through in a single year 200 shirts, 37 hats, between 65 and 146 pairs of hose, 60 pairs of socks and 175 pairs of satin shoes, velvet slippers and leather boots. His finest embroidered shirts were given as New Year's gifts and his daily linen sewn for him by the wives of humbler courtiers. Katherine of Aragon lovingly made him shirts – even after he had told her that their marriage was over. Anne Boleyn refused, hiring a shirt maker instead.[2]

Henry was a conspicuous consumer of art and culture rather than a genuine connoisseur like Francis I of France. He accumulated things chiefly because he could – and he did so indiscriminately, acquiring the costliest items more as stage props than for their intrinsic appeal. Visiting dignitaries would be given conducted tours of his treasures. Occasionally he showed them off to the public. In 1527, he threw open the doors of a temporary banqueting house at Greenwich for three or four days, so that 'all honest persons' could admire a display of his most prized tapestries, along with two gigantic cupboards stacked high with his finest gold and silver plate.[3]

Henry kept smaller collectors' objects in his private studies or in cabinets in the privy galleries at his palaces. Among them were exotic items such as *pietre dure* cups and jugs, Venetian glass, alabaster figures and table 'jewels' created as conversation pieces. These might include fish, birds, boats, scallops or snails made of rock crystal or mother-of-pearl, set with gold or silver, rubies, diamonds and pearls. Also kept in cabinets were perfume, spice or pepper boxes made of gold or ebony, and miniatures and cameo portraits such as 'a picture of Prince Edward's face graven in agate set in gold'. Other cherished items were mechanical devices, notably watches and chiming clocks. Two of his clocks were in the shape of dogs, for Henry had his pets. Whenever two of his favourite greyhounds, Ball and Cut, went missing, people who returned them would be handsomely rewarded.[4]

As a young man, Henry spent less on buildings and art treasures than he did in later life. Before Wolsey reshaped his tastes, they were inspired more by his adolescent dreams of the Knights of the Round Table and the Arthurian legends. It was in these same years that he ordered the Round Table at Winchester – which as a teenager he had proudly shown off to his hero Philip the Handsome – to be fully repaired and repainted.[5]

Things changed rapidly when Wolsey taught him how to refurbish his palaces or to build new ones with continental amenities such as loggias and long galleries, and then fill them with quality artworks.[6] In 1516, Henry began construction works at Beaulieu (or New Hall) in Essex, also taking over Wolsey's London house of Bridewell and turning it into a new city palace. Soon Wolsey would be project-managing major building works for Henry at Greenwich, Eltham, the Savoy Hospital and elsewhere, while running a massive parallel operation at his own properties – chiefly at Hampton Court, York Place beside Westminster and The More (now Moor Park) near Rickmansworth in Hertfordshire.[7]

In 1518, Henry first began to plan a magnificent marble mausoleum for himself in the Lady Chapel at St George's Chapel, Windsor: one that would be heroic in its awe-inspiring grandeur and outshine his father's at Westminster Abbey.[8] Wolsey declared that only a Florentine sculptor would be up to the task, and Pope Leo, a patron of Raphael and Michelangelo, was brought in to trawl for suitable candidates. By 1521, the choice lay between Michelangelo and an inferior rival. But Michelangelo could not be chosen, because the pope preferred to keep him in Rome and so new candidates were sought.

So insistent was Henry for the pope's verdict that Leo hauled himself from his bed on the night before his death to examine a scale model of one of the proposed designs, showing 142 life-sized figures in bronze lining the stairs around the sepulchre, a life-size sculpture of Henry on horseback looking down on the scene, and the whole framed by a massive triumphal arch with carved pillars and bronze relief panels. Two alternative designs were subsequently considered, and – with Leo in his grave and Michelangelo busy with the Medici funerary chapel in Florence – models of all three were brought to Henry at Greenwich in February 1523. But no commission would be placed: the king would be preoccupied with war and diplomacy for the next four years, and then his divorce suit intervened.[9]

In 1530, Benedetto da Rovezzano and his assistant Giovanni da Maiano, both of whom had travelled to England from Florence in 1519 to help complete the altar for Henry VII's Chapel at Westminster Abbey, were at last contracted to begin Henry's mausoleum – but to yet another design.

Da Rovezzano proposed remodelling and greatly enlarging for Henry the nucleus of a colossal black and white marble monument that since 1524 he had been creating for the now disgraced Wolsey. Complete with an altar and large bronze reliefs and surrounded by columns 9 feet high topped by gilt-bronze candlesticks born by angels, the work was almost finished in 1543. But by then, da Rovezzano was sixty-nine. With his health poor and his eyesight failing, he decided to return to Florence: the unassembled tomb was left still in pieces on the floor at his workshop.[10]

In Henry's lifetime, the art treasures most consistently coveted by continental rulers were Flemish tapestries, especially those woven from preliminary cartoons by famous Italian artists. Once more Wolsey pointed the way, and by the time of the meeting with Francis I at the Field of Cloth of Gold in 1520, Henry had purchased over 170 high-quality Flemish works to add to the 450 or so less expensive wall hangings he had inherited.[11]

Thus far, Henry had been content merely to keep pace with Wolsey as a collector, but when he began to question the cardinal's abilities and was goading him into action over his first divorce, he went much further, setting out to rival the pope himself in pomp and show. His opening move was to commission the first of a series of breathtakingly expensive gold-woven tapestry sets of a similar quality to those commissioned by Pope Leo in the first two years of his pontificate from cartoons by Raphael and his workshop. Just one of Henry's orders placed in 1528 for a ten-piece tapestry set, *The Story of King David*, was the largest and most opulent of the day outside Rome, with a surface area of just under 420 square yards.[12]

Tapestries were relatively portable. With care, they could be moved from one palace to another and rehung, enabling Henry with relative ease to redecorate specific rooms to suit his requirements, or else to illustrate particular classical, chivalric or biblical themes in keeping with the subjects of impending dramatic or musical entertainments. Commissioning or rearranging panel portraits or statuary around a specific theme was another approach he took to interior design. During the 1540s, a fine collection of dynastic portraits of European and English rulers, including of Henry himself and his parents and grandparents, was on permanent display in the gallery at St James's Palace. This imitated a decorative scheme devised at Richmond by Henry VII, where the walls of the great hall were lined with statues of English warrior kings, beginning with Hengist of Kent and King Arthur and ending with the victor of Bosworth himself.[13]

Besides new purchases in the years before and after he broke with Rome, Henry added extensively to his art collections through forfeitures of the property of convicted traitors that the law allowed, or through plundering the abbeys. Significant confiscations had begun in 1521, after the Duke of Buckingham was beheaded. Among the vast haul from Buckingham's houses and estates were the duke's ancestral castle at Thornbury in Gloucestershire, expensively remodelled as a castellated luxury home, and his many fine-quality tapestries, several woven with silk and gold or silver thread.

Wolsey's fall added even richer booty, including the great

Thamesside house of York Place (which the king renamed Whitehall and made his own preferred city palace) and 600 tapestries. Cartloads of cash, jewels, gold and silver plate, precious fabrics and items of furniture were carried off for Henry's use or else stored in the ground-floor offices of the Royal Wardrobe, with the rest mothballed wherever space could be found.[14]

Portraits were not at first much in vogue in Henry's reign, but the Augsburg-born portraitist Hans Holbein the Younger changed all that. Holbein first arrived in England in 1526 from his adopted city of Basel bearing a letter of introduction to Thomas More. For the entertainment of the French ambassadors at Greenwich in 1527, Holbein painted a spectacular battle scene on the back of a triumphal arch and constructed with his friend, the astronomer Nicholas Kratzer, a sensational trompe-l'œil ceiling for a purpose-built theatre. The artist also painted Thomas More and his family, in particular the superlative portrait of More now in the Frick Collection in New York and a linen wall hanging of a life-size family-group scene for his house at Chelsea.[15]

During Holbein's second visit, in the 1530s, Cromwell – another noted art connoisseur – sat for his portrait. Then, in 1535, he steered the artist in a different direction, commissioning a folio woodcut for the title page of Miles Coverdale's Bible translation. In it, Henry is seated on his throne in majesty, wearing his closed or 'imperial' crown and carrying the sword of state while distributing God's Word to his bishops and nobles. The Hebrew letters spelling the name of God are placed at the top of the page. The image of Henry positioned directly beneath signifies the king's special status as Christ's deputy on earth. And on either side of the page, a series of panels depicting scenes from the Old and New Testament flags up Henry's new-found emphasis on the 'Word of God' as a 'super-sacrament'.[16]

Whereas Cromwell could see at a glance the value of Holbein's art as propaganda, Henry did not fully wake up to the artist's potential until as late as 1537, when he gave Holbein the title of 'the king's painter' and commissioned him to rebrand the monarchy to match his new status as Supreme Head of the Church. Holbein's first task was to fresco a life-size dynastic mural for the Privy Chamber at Whitehall. Some 12 feet by 9 feet, and painted on the central portion of the north wall, the mural was designed to create the illusion of a three-dimensional space and to mirror the king's reflected glory to those entering the room. It depicted Henry standing, legs astride, on a rich Turkish carpet in front of his father, with Jane Seymour in front of Elizabeth of York on the other side of the tableau.[17] Positioned to face Henry's throne on the opposite side of the room, the mural was destroyed with much of the palace itself in a fire in 1698 and is now known only through a small copy made for Charles II and from the surviving lefthand section of Holbein's cartoon used for transferring the composition to the wall.[18]

By the time the fresco was completed, Jane Seymour was already dead. In fact, her death changed nothing, since by giving Henry the legitimate male heir he so desired, she became the wife he most wanted to memorialize. But that was not the only unusual thing. In the background of the mural Holbein created richly coloured, trompe-l'œil vaulting above the surrounding colonnade, complete with deep arches, 'antique' cornice work and classical figures, all taken from an architectural print by Bernardo Prevedari, after Donato Bramante, the Italian painter and architect most famous for his plans for the rebuilding of St Peter's in Rome. What Henry never knew, however, was that the centrepiece of Prevedari's original print had been a tonsured monk who, oblivious to the bystanders, kneels before an elevated crucifix. Undoubtedly this was Holbein's secret joke.

In the course of reviewing a preliminary version of Holbein's cartoon for the mural, Henry insisted on being repositioned full-face to the viewer rather than three-quarter face. The result – rare for Holbein, as at the time it was considered vulgar – is that he stares straight out at us. Henry intended the Whitehall mural to show that he had no physical deformities. A virtuoso realization of the heroic presence of God's anointed king – as well as of Henry's physical eligibility as a husband at a time when he was already searching for a new wife – the image was so realistic that those who saw it reported that they had been 'stricken with fear' when they first approached it. For it seemed as if Holbein's subjects were physically present in the room.[19]

But the viewer's eye would have been drawn not just to Henry, but to the stone monument, often mistakenly said to be an altar, at the centre of the composition on which the king's father, Henry VII, casually rested his left arm. Carved on it was an inscription in Latin verse, which recalls the debate about how to perpetuate a ruler's fame and reputation, a debate that went back to the time of Apelles, court painter to Philip of Macedon and his son Alexander the Great. The question was: 'Which glorifies a ruler more enduringly, a painting or an inscription carved in stone?'

Rather than choose between the two, Henry had Holbein deliver both – a dynastic portrait with a monument at its focal point on which the inscription read (when translated):

If you find pleasure in seeing fair pictures of heroes,
Look then at these! None greater was ever portrayed.
Fierce is the struggle and hot the disputing: the question [is],
Does the father, or does the son – or do both – have the
    pre-eminence?
One ever withstood his enemies and his country's
    destruction,
At last giving his people the blessing of peace.

But the son, born to greater things, drove out of his councils
His worthless ministers and ever supported the just.
And in truth, the overweening power of the Pope bowed to
    his resolve,
When the sceptre of power was wielded by Henry VIII,
Under whose reign the true religion was restored to the
    nation
And pure doctrine began to be held in honour.[20]

In other words, Henry is the greatest king who ever lived, the only one equal to his God-given mission for the renovation of Church and State, the only one capable of achievements that could outshine his father's in creating the dynasty.

Holbein next painted an exquisite miniature on vellum of

King Solomon receiving the homage of the Queen of Sheba. The painting was executed in grisaille with extensive touches of gold, the only colour coming from an azurite background and the single, evocative detail of the red and green of the strawberries offered to Solomon.

The figure of Solomon is a lifelike portrait of Henry. The Queen of Sheba was a traditional emblem of the Church, so the painting illustrated Henry as Supreme Head receiving the homage of the Church of England. The cloth of estate behind his throne bears a Latin inscription based on verses from the Old Testament (I Kings 10:9, II Chronicles 9:7–8), proclaiming that Henry is appointed directly by, and is accountable only to, God. And on the steps of the throne is inscribed: 'By your virtues you have exceeded your reputation.'[21]

Through the medium of this miniature, Holbein further redefined Henry's image to reflect the king's understanding of himself, depicting him as a patriarch in a covenant with God. Via representations such as this, Henry was not just said but *seen* to be a second King Solomon – who, by expelling the pope and idolatry from his dominions and reappropriating the 'true' powers of the monarchy, had finished 'the building of the Temple' begun by his father, Henry VII.

Finally, Holbein and his assistants painted a series of panel portraits and diptychs in various sizes of Henry and Jane Seymour, modelled on the cartoon for the Whitehall mural and its preliminary drawings. By far the most impressive of these is Holbein's commonly reproduced half-length portrait of Henry now in the Thyssen-Bornemisza Collection in Madrid. Here, he is positioned three-quarter face, dressed in a high-necked doublet of cloth of silver and gold that is studded with jewels, wearing a feathered cap and carrying a glove in his right hand.

Holbein knew just how to work his magic. In 1539, as a New Year's gift, the artist presented Henry with a 'table [meaning an oak panel] of the picture of the prince's grace' – a portrait of the fifteen-month-old Edward, the king's sole legitimate male heir. It was the ideal subject for a gift, prompting Henry to reward Holbein with a solid gold cup in return.[22]

But the image is of no ordinary toddler. In the painting the prince looks a year or two older, totally self-assured, and, like the king in the mural, is shown full-face to the viewer. The child wears a gold-embroidered red tunic with cloth of gold sleeves, and on his head he sports a red velvet cap, trimmed with silver and gold, with an ostrich feather to the side. In his left hand he holds a golden rattle like a sceptre and raises his right hand, fingers outstretched, as if in blessing. This is the Supreme Head of the Church in waiting.[23]

Since even a toddler had to propagate the Tudor brand, the prince's portrait came with another revealing Latin verse inscription:

Little one, emulate your father and be the heir of his virtue; the world contains nothing greater. Heaven and earth could scarcely produce a son whose glory would surpass that of such a father. Only equal the deeds of your parent and men can wish for no more. Surpass him and you have surpassed all the kings the world ever revered and none will surpass you.[24]

Composed by Richard Morison, one of Cromwell's pro-
tégés, the verse was clearly directed more at the father than
the child. It ranked Henry's immortal fame as rivalling or
excelling that of heroes like Alexander the Great, just as
Erasmus had suggested in 1499 when he first met the young
Henry on his visit to the royal schoolroom with Thomas
More.

Almost singlehandedly, Holbein achieved for Henry what
chivalry, expensive building projects, extravagant dress and
tapestry purchases had failed to do. No other artist available
in England could match Holbein's genius, but with the plundered wealth of the abbeys now enriching the royal coffers,
that did not stop Henry. In his final years, he revealed the
full extent of the legend he sought to leave behind by commissioning tapestry sets that showed how he identified
himself with key biblical role models in an intensely personal way. Not content with acquiring one or two sets of
The Story of King David, he ended up with nine. Just as he
had already come to associate himself with David's son
Solomon, so he came to imagine himself as David too, and
when the artist and poet Jean Mallard, an émigré from the
court of Francis I, presented him with a sumptuously illustrated psalter in 1540, the miniature images he had created
of David were lifelike portraits of Henry.[25]

Henry, then, came to feel a close affinity with David,
believing he had liberated England from the great Goliath
of papal tyranny. God's anointed ruler of his chosen people
and a famous warrior, David had restored the Ark of the
Covenant to Jerusalem and attacked false idols. Like David,
Henry was an author and musician. Like him, too, he

believed he had shown magnanimity to his enemies. In the Hebrew tradition, David's house and dominions were to stand for ever. And not only this: for his transgressions, David was punished by God with the death of his first child, just as Henry saw himself as being punished in 1511 for marrying his brother's widow by the loss of young Prince Henry, Katherine of Aragon's baby.

In a striking act of cultural appropriation in 1540, Henry commissioned for Whitehall Palace a duplicate set of the remarkable tapestry series known as the *Acts of the Apostles*, depicting scenes from the lives of St Peter and St Paul, that Pope Leo had commissioned in 1515 from cartoons by Raphael to cover the lower walls of the Sistine Chapel at the Vatican. Ranked equal in price and quality with the pope's set and made by the same weavers, Henry's purchase showed how far he had come to view himself as the new pope in England.[26] He then trumped this with the costliest of all his commissions, a ten-piece set of tapestries, *The Story of Abraham*, woven largely of silk and gilt-metal thread. Based on scenes depicting the main events of Abraham's life as recorded in the Book of Genesis, the chief themes related to Abraham's role as the founder of the Hebrew nation and the continuation of God's covenant with him through his son Isaac. For Abraham read Henry, and for Isaac read young Prince Edward.[27] Henry's fascination with the theme is further documented by the generous reward he gave in 1544 to Nicholas Bellin of Modena – a noted Italian painter and designer who now worked extensively for him – for presenting him on New Year's Day with a panel painting (now lost) entitled *A Story of Abraham*.[28]

Recently poached from Francis I – he had been working on a new gallery at Fontainebleau – Bellin became the chief impresario of Henry's culturally most ambitious building project, Nonsuch Palace in Surrey, so called because in Tudor speech 'nonsuch' meant 'second to none'. Designed as a summer retreat where the king could go with his queen and a privileged group of courtiers to hunt and relax, the structure was timber-framed, with two great octagonal towers at the outer corners on the south front.[29] Adapting techniques he had perfected at Fontainebleau, Bellin used stucco designs framed by 'slate' panels made of black, fine-grained limestone to adorn the bricks between the timbers. Nowhere was this more expertly done than on the exterior surfaces of the east and west walls of the Inner Court. From almost ground to roof level, Bellin filled in the spaces between the windows with symmetrical rows of terracotta heads of Roman emperors, stucco images of gods and goddesses, panels representing the story of the Labours of Hercules, the Seven Liberal Arts, the four Cardinal Virtues, and so on.[30]

But Nonsuch differed from Fontainebleau in one key respect. Presiding over the scene from the centre of the south side of the court were life-sized statues of Henry, seated on an ivory throne, with Prince Edward beside him. Like Solomon, the pair were judges of all they surveyed. And to ensure that no one missed the point, Henry trampled a lion beneath his feet, an unmistakable reference to his victory over the pope.

Had, however, Holbein lived to see Henry's death, he would have had the last laugh. Like Thomas More and his fellow art connoisseurs, Holbein knew when a sitter's motives were base. Henry may have wanted to go down in history as an Old Testament patriarch and the new pope in England, but in the king's most celebrated three-quarter-face portrait, his features are cold and threatening and his piggy eyes glower with suspicion. He seems blissfully unaware that portraits – by Holbein's rules – can 'talk' to us. Their function was to depict 'the figure and similitude' of the sitter's soul rather than 'the features of his body'.[31]

Thus in his portrait of Jane Seymour, for all her jewels and the sumptuousness of her gown, Holbein shows us that her mouth is mean, the look on her face blank and expressionless. She appears to us as every bit the queen who climbed over another's corpse to win her place. His classic portrait of Henry, in particular, suggests that he had grasped to perfection the psyche of a man who could declare with pride: 'By God, I trust no one but myself.'[32] Henry always liked to believe he was an 'affable prince', but Holbein's haunting images depict his Court as a world of terror and uncertainty. They were an ideal medium for conveying what no one else dared say.

6
Epilogue

By the spring of 1538, the ulcer on Henry's left leg had considerably worsened and he could be laid up in agony for up to twelve days at a stretch. He would turn black in the face and become speechless if the passageway in the skin through which the pus escaped closed up, obliging his physicians to cut open, cauterize and freshly bandage it.[1] Shortly before he landed at Calais to lead the siege of Boulogne, at the age of fifty-three, it was said that 'he has the worst legs in the world' – so much so that 'those who have seen him of late wonder how it is that he does not keep to his bed'.[2] To aid his mobility, he ordered a set of walking staffs and was painted holding one of them in his left hand. He carried a whistle as a means to summon help and had two 'trunks to shout in', possibly a primitive form of megaphone.[3]

On returning from the siege of Boulogne in 1544, he lived and worked chiefly in his private studies, hiding himself away within the secret lodgings of his palaces. To spare him walking from room to room or along the galleries at his largest palace, Whitehall, he commissioned two purpose-built movable chairs known as 'trams', each covered in tawny velvet and with a matching footstool.[4] A special commode was made for him, the exterior covered in black velvet held in place by 2,000 gilded nails and with the seat and arms stuffed with prodigious quantities of down.[5] A third movable chair was covered with russet velvet, and finally a more complex contraption was devised, quilted with purple silk, 'which goeth up and down'.[6] Charles V's ambassador saw him being carried around Windsor Castle in one of these chairs, and shortly afterwards Bess Holland, the Duke of Norfolk's mistress, reported that her lover had told her that the king 'was much grown of his body, and that he could not go up and down the stairs, but was let up and down by a device'.[7]

Despite his bodily infirmities, Henry refused to give up hunting completely. He had abandoned riding to hounds years before. Now, he shot from a stand with longbows, crossbows or muskets at the deer and birds that beaters trapped or caught in nets and released for him into a fenced enclosure. To this end, he purchased a large number of expensively decorated firearms. His approach was much deplored by Francis I, who maintained it was unchivalrous to use firearms against defenceless animals.[8]

The modern experts who hypothesize that haemolytic disease of the newborn caused the pregnancy failures of Henry's first two queens also argue that in later life he suffered from a rare genetic disorder known as McLeod syndrome. A condition almost exclusive to males that develops around the age of forty, this syndrome is associated with neurological and psychiatric disorders such as muscle weakness and nerve deterioration especially in the lower limbs, coupled with recurring bouts of depression, paranoia and irrational personality changes.[9]

But Henry's obesity is in itself sufficient to explain much of his physical and mental decline. It is far more likely that obesity-mediated type 2 diabetes caused peripheral neuropathy, with resulting muscular failure and difficulty in walking, worsening his leg ulcers and accompanied (as Anne Boleyn had begun to notice) by erectile dysfunction and behavioural disturbances. Symptoms of possible diabetes include the king's heavy drinking and restless sleeping patterns caused by his inability to urinate effectively.

A high-protein diet was alone responsible for his constant and painful constipation. The royal kitchen accounts show that for over thirty years he had consumed a dozen or more portions of meat, fowl or fish in two courses for dinner and nearly as much again for supper, with custard or fritters for pudding and only very small amounts of fruit or vegetables. Only the finest-quality white bread was served at his table, along with prodigious quantities of red wine and ale.[10]

As to the treatments that he routinely received, the monthly accounts of his apothecaries prove that – plasters, bandages and other emollients for his ulcerated legs and burning skin apart – the bulk of the drugs administered to him were diuretics to promote urine production, laxatives and enemas to relieve constipation, pills or lozenges for indigestion and ointments for haemorrhoids. Since none of his medicaments included mercury – the basis of the standard treatment for venereal diseases in his lifetime – syphilis can confidently be ruled out.[11]

Vivid evidence exists of the melancholy, anxieties and suspicions that afflicted Henry in his declining years.

Charles's ambassador reported that he would dress to go to Mass or to sit in his privy garden and then instead stay put, brooding over what the French or the Scots were plotting.[12] When his legs swelled and gave him unbearable pain, he grew even more suspicious than usual of disloyalty and muttered dark misgivings about his councillors and subjects, whom he threatened to 'make so poor that they would not have the boldness nor the power to oppose him'.[13]

In the interval between Anne Boleyn's fall and Cromwell's, the courtier-poet and royal ambassador to Spain, Thomas Wyatt – himself in the Tower within a whisker of execution in 1541 on a charge of treasonable intelligence with Reginald Pole – had written verses depicting Henry's palaces as a gilded cage. Reflecting on the Old Testament history of David in his paraphrases of the penitential Psalms, Wyatt characterized the biblical king as a troubled tyrant touched by Satan. From lust he had degenerated to idolatry, from idolatry to murder, and from murder to an abject search for penitence. He at last repents, renouncing 'triumph and conquest' – but his spiritual pilgrimage can find no end.[14]

In Henry's case, such a pilgrimage did not even begin. By 1545, he was exhibiting clear signs of paranoia. One sign was that he encouraged spies and informers to intercept his courtiers' private letters.[15] Other signals came from his letters to his ambassadors abroad: they complained that he kept his intentions secret to the point where they were unable to do their jobs.[16]

More poignantly, his treatment of his sixth wife, Katherine Parr, shows his obsession with controlling even those he claimed most to love. A convert to the evangelical reform movement, Katherine (like Anne Boleyn) read the writings of the religious reformers in French and dared to discuss them with her husband at mealtimes.[17]

Henry, however, had persuaded Parliament in 1543 to restrict who was allowed to read the Bible other than the Latin Vulgate edition on a status and gender basis, fearing that the Bible translations he had so far authorized were fuelling heresy and sectarian dissent.[18] Noblewomen were still allowed to study the Bible privately, but not to discuss their opinions with others – so Katherine knew she had to be careful.[19] Occasionally she let her guard down: early in 1546, Henry openly showed his irritation at what he considered to be her 'meddling' in religion. This set off the backstairs whisperers, and within weeks articles would be drawn up by her enemies charging her with heresy, which the king signed, possibly in a fit of pique.[20]

Oblivious to the danger, Katherine carried on as usual – until the eve of her planned arrest, when her husband dropped a hint of what was to come to one of his physicians. In what quickly developed into a black comedy, a copy of the articles, with his signature, was then 'accidentally' dropped where she would find it. Terrified and nearly hysterical, she feigned sickness and retreated to her bed-chamber. There Henry came to her, which given his renowned aversion to visiting the sick or confronting those he was intent on destroying suggests a deliberate intrigue to teach his wife a lesson.[21]

If so, she played her part to perfection and so kept her head, sitting on his lap next day and – like Shakespeare's

Katharina in *The Taming of the Shrew* – declaring herself to be but 'a silly poor woman' while her husband was 'my only anchor, Supreme Head and Governor here on earth, next unto God'.

With a sure grasp of Henry's psychology, Katherine then touched him on the points on which he was most vulnerable – his health and his vanity. If she had inadvertently 'meddled', she declared, it was not to advance her own opinions, but merely to distract him from his sickness, so that she, 'hearing your majesty's earnest discourse, might receive to myself some profit thereby'.

'And is it even so, sweetheart,' he replied, suitably mollified. 'Then perfect friends are we now again.' Whereupon he threw his arms around her and kissed her, afterwards showering her with gifts of jewels, furs and clothes in the very latest fashions.[22]

Before leaving for Boulogne, Henry had asked Parliament to enact his final succession settlement. The Act determined – assuming Katherine Parr bore him no children – that the throne would pass to Edward, then Mary and finally to Elizabeth, with the restriction that their father might specify conditions for the succession of each of his daughters in his last will and testament.[23]

For Henry, the idea of a female on the throne was only marginally more palatable in 1544 than it had been twenty years previously, when he had invested his illegitimate son, Henry Fitzroy, as Duke of Richmond and Somerset. He continued to see the kingship claims of his daughters' potential husbands as a serious problem, and was determined to tackle it. Before long, he would spell out what was to happen if either of his daughters married without the consent of the councillors he would name – she would lose her place. And if both were disqualified, then the throne would pass, in turn, to the heirs of his nieces, the Ladies Frances and Eleanor Brandon, the daughters of his younger sister, Mary, who had married the Duke of Suffolk as her second husband. Should this so-called 'Suffolk line' fail, then the throne was to go to the 'next rightful heirs'.[24]

When, as death approached, Henry finally revised his will, no provision was made for the appointment of a single person to act as a Lord Protector. Instead, he appointed sixteen privy councillors to govern in his son's name until the boy was eighteen. Twelve other individuals were to assist and be 'of counsel' to them, ensuring stability and a political consensus during the young king's minority.[25]

Since Edward was still only nine, the question of who would take power and rule in practice came to dominate the minds and ambitions of the ailing king's entourage. Shortly before the peace with France in 1546, matters had begun to move towards a dénouement when, following defeat in a skirmish, the Earl of Surrey was relieved of his command at Boulogne and replaced by the Earl of Hertford. Deeply unpopular with Henry's councillors for encouraging the king to retain Boulogne against all financial and military odds, Surrey's card had been marked.

In the ensuing struggle for power, Surrey and his father, the Duke of Norfolk, aligned themselves against Hertford and his close ally William Paget, the king's secretary. Norfolk and Surrey represented all that was 'old' in Henry's reign – in tradition, in religion and (at least, as far as the duke – now in his seventies – was concerned) in age. Hertford and Paget – supported from the wings by Sir Anthony Denny, the chief gentleman of Henry's Privy Chamber – represented the 'new': crucially, they and not their rivals surrounded the increasingly secluded king on a daily basis.[26]

Norfolk and Surrey were hopelessly outmanoeuvred. An accomplished poet and erstwhile friend of Thomas Wyatt whose epitaph he wrote, Surrey had also proved himself to be a capable soldier and courtier. But he was recklessly ambitious, jealously proud of his descent from both Edward I and Edward III and openly contemptuous of the 'erected' (i.e. self-made) men like Hertford and Paget, all of which clouded his judgement. On 2 December 1546, Surrey was arrested and taken to Lord Chancellor Wriothesley's house in Holborn, where he was interrogated. Ten days later, he was marched unceremoniously through the streets of London and thrown into the Tower. Stripped of his offices and Order of the Garter, his father, Norfolk, was taken by river to the same fortress on the same day.[27]

Since Surrey had already fallen from royal favour, it was comparatively easy for Hertford and Paget to complete his demise. The earl was his own worst enemy, with his hubris, his rash, overbearing claims to a royal lineage, his beliefs in the power of the old nobility and his alleged remark that his father the duke was the 'rightful' claimant to the position of Protector of the boy-king.[28] Put on trial on trumped-up treason charges in January 1547, Surrey was quickly found guilty and beheaded.[29] The main allegation was that he had wrongfully included the arms of Edward the Confessor in his own coat of arms, which it was alleged challenged Henry's right to the throne and made more likely the 'peril' of a future insurrection like the Pilgrimage of Grace. That Surrey in fact had every right to display these arms on account of his noble descent was swept aside.[30]

His father was more difficult to handle. To destroy him, Hertford and Paget simply lied, telling Henry that the duke and his son were in a conspiracy to murder all of the Council and seize control of Edward, just as Richard III had seized control of Edward IV's young sons in 1483.[31] This, indeed, is what foreign ambassadors were told. The nature of the allegations meant that Henry closely followed every detail of the ensuing interrogations from his sickbed, his handwritten annotations littering the questions and possible charges being framed against the accused. Obsessed with securing the dynasty and the life of his young son, and remembering all too well the crisis in the last years of his own father's reign after Prince Arthur's death, he was so caught up in trying to direct history that he failed to see that what was really happening around him amounted to a coup d'état.[32]

Condemned by act of Parliament without trial for concealing his son's offence, Norfolk would be spared only because Henry's death preceded by a few hours the time set for his execution. The royal assent to the duke's attainder was given in the House of Lords by proxy on 27 January 1547, when Wriothesley explained that Henry was too ill to attend.[33] Norfolk was to have been beheaded at 9 a.m. on Friday the 28th, but by the previous evening, the king lay slipping in and out of consciousness in a massively enlarged bed that had been made for him at Whitehall. It was clear that his end was very near and Archbishop Cranmer, the only surviving churchman to retain the king's absolute trust, was sent for.

By the time he arrived, Henry had lost the power of speech. Seeing he was too far gone to make his confession, Cranmer told him to make some sign or gesture that he 'put his trust in Christ and called on his mercy'. Henry responded by 'holding him with his hand' and then 'did wring his hand in his as hard as he could'. Shortly afterwards, between midnight and 1 o'clock in the morning, the king died, aged fifty-five.[34]

Only Denny, Cranmer and some of the royal physicians are known to have been present. But Hertford and Paget, if not in the bedchamber at the moment Henry died, were certainly within earshot, whispering about their plans for the future in a nearby gallery.[35] Neither Katherine Parr nor the king's children were allowed access, although a scribbled note to one of his daughters (we do not know which) suggests that Henry had not completely forgotten them.[36] 'Mine own good daughter,' it said, 'I pray you remember me most heartily when you in your prayers do pray for grace to be attained assuredly to your loving father.'[37] They may be among the last words he ever wrote.

In a macabre replay of the bedchamber crisis that had followed his father's death at Richmond in 1509, the news of Henry's passing was kept secret for three days. During that period of limbo, 'not the slightest signs ... were to be seen at Court, and even the usual ceremony of bearing in the royal dishes to the sounds of trumpets was continued without interruption'.[38]

Behind the scenes, however, Hertford was busy. After a tense exchange with his fellow councillors and with Paget's help, his coup succeeded and he set out for Hertford Castle where Edward was staying, in order to bring him to the Tower ready for his coronation.[39] For some time, members of the Council had been meeting chiefly at Hertford's house. Now, for greater secrecy, they met at the Tower, where shortly afterwards they would also take the decision to make Hertford Lord Protector and Duke of Somerset. But Hertford could not command a majority to renew the warrant for Norfolk's execution; instead, the duke was left to rot in the Tower for the whole of Edward's reign.[40]

Once Hertford had Edward safely under his control, Lord Chancellor Wriothesley, in floods of tears, announced Henry's death to Parliament. Before leaving the capital, members of the House of Lords were summoned to Edward's Presence Chamber at the Tower to hear the old king's will read by Paget.[41] Then the heralds proclaimed Edward king.

The royal embalmers, meanwhile, prepared Henry's body for his funeral. Carried in great pomp on a chariot to St George's Chapel, Windsor, for the interment, the lead coffin encased in elm 2 inches thick was lowered next to the body of Jane Seymour in the plain vault in the middle of the choir between the stalls and the altar.

In his will, Henry had expressed his desire to be buried with Jane in the grand mausoleum he had once planned for the Lady Chapel, but the marble and bronze pieces still lay, unassembled, on the floor of Benedetto da Rovezzano's old workshop. Moved to the Lady Chapel in 1565, they were stacked there until 1646, when the bronze was sold to pay the Windsor garrison. Of the original bronze work, only four large candlesticks and four candle-bearing angels still survive.[42] In 1808, the marble sarcophagus and pedestal were recycled by the government for Lord Nelson's tomb in the crypt of St Paul's.[43]

In the 1590s, Sir Francis Englefield – a junior diplomat on the mission to negotiate Henry's peace treaty with France in 1546 – boasted in exile to his Catholic friends that during Mary Tudor's reign he had been one of a hand-picked team of courtiers who had exhumed Henry's body from its final resting place at the request of Reginald Pole, and had it burned to ashes.[44] Although often still repeated, the story is entirely false: when the vault was opened in 1813 in the presence of the Prince Regent, Henry's skeleton was seen to be still very much intact. Some beard was even visible on the chin.[45]

From his earliest days, Henry had sought fame and recognition. And to a great extent he succeeded. Besides successfully defying the pope, he redefined the powers of the monarchy, enlarged the horizons of Parliament and established the Church of England, giving them the broad shape they would retain for the next four hundred years. He sincerely believed himself to be Christ's deputy on earth. He lived and breathed the role, even imagining that he could ordain bishops and priests.[46] In diplomacy he rivalled the King of France and at times the Holy Roman Emperor. With Wolsey and Holbein's help, he dragged England into the mainstream of the artistic Renaissance. He even attempted (if unsuccessfully) to bridge the wider Reformation divide.

His material legacy was astonishing. Inheriting no more than a dozen palaces and greater houses from his father, he left 55 to his son, filled with over 2,000 tapestries, 150 or more panel paintings, 2,028 items of gold and silver plate and 1,780 books.[47] His arsenals were as well stocked as his palaces. He equipped the chain of fortresses he built along the south coast with 2,250 pieces of artillery, and with 400 or so more guns and 6,500 muskets in reserve at the Tower.[48] By the time he made peace with France in 1546, he had some 50 royal navy ships in active service and another 21 in need of repair. For all this, he was confidently judged by his contemporaries to be the equal of the Roman emperors Hadrian and Justinian.

Henry held deep convictions and had a genuine desire to change Christendom for the better both before and after he quarrelled with the pope. As a younger man, he was relatively open to advice, but this changed radically in middle age. While he could be lazy and inattentive, when matters touched him deeply he had an astonishing capacity for work. In preparing his suit for divorce from Katherine of Aragon, he was an especially attentive reader. On the title page of Thomas Abell's *Invicta Veritas* ('Unconquerable Truth'), written in Katherine's favour, he jotted 'Fundamentum huius libri vanum est' ('The basic premise of this book is worthless'). In the margin of his copy of *Summa de Potestate Ecclesiastica* ('A Compendium Concerning Ecclesiastical Power') by Augustine of Ancona, a late thirteenth-century papal theorist, he scribbled in delight 'Ergo nec in nobis' ('Therefore neither in ours') on encountering the words 'First, therefore, it must be said that to have several wives was not against nature in the ancient fathers'.[49] Where leagues or treaties were concerned, he had a highly retentive memory and a keen eye for detail. Few English monarchs before or since could rival his mastery of the minutiae, which he could recall at the drop of a hat many years later.

When, in December 1545, Henry addressed Parliament for the very last time, he made an impassioned plea for unity and concord in the realm, chiefly in religion, drawing his leading subjects together in a way that would not be seen again until Elizabeth I made her famous speech to her troops at Tilbury at the time of the Spanish Armada in 1588. One enthralled listener said that the king spoke 'with such a gravity, so sententiously, so kingly, or rather fatherly' to his subjects that grown men wept. 'To us that have not heard him often, [it] was such a joy and marvellous comfort, as I reckon this day one of the happiest of my life.'[50]

On the other side of the ledger, Henry plundered the abbeys and wasted much of the proceeds in war or on extravagant building works far in excess of his needs. His summer palace at Nonsuch may have been England's Fontainebleau, but Henry could never find an adequate water source nearby, and so stayed there only twice. To pay for his defence of Boulogne and later campaigns in Scotland, he levied taxes and debased the coinage without regard for the economic effects. Most notably, Thomas More, John Fisher and the Carthusian priors were vindictively pursued and judicially murdered after what amounted to show trials for what were little more than crimes of the mind.

Bullying and hectoring those around him, Henry always had to be in the right. For days or weeks he would brood over what he considered to be slights, however trivial. In his desire for his dynasty's security and faced by menacing threats from abroad after he was excommunicated, he was forever suspecting plots to topple him. In the 1530s, fear of Yorkist conspiracy as represented by Reginald Pole and his relatives was linked in his mind to fear of papal conspiracy. By the closing months of the reign when he turned on the Earl of Surrey and his father, the atmosphere at Court was as claustrophobic and inward-looking as anything in the final years of his father's reign, with courtiers and servants alike fearing spies and informers.

Blessed with an elastic, self-serving conscience teaching him that what he found to be expedient must by definition be just, Henry had an unerring talent for swiftly redefining friends and loyal servants as traitors if they disappointed him. He could turn vengefully on those who thwarted or contradicted him – such as his first two wives and Thomas More – and did so with a terrifying, irrational ferocity. At the same time, he deluded himself that he had treated them well. He convinced himself that they were 'ungrateful' and 'disobedient' and had returned his love with 'uncharitable' contempt.[51]

After he had broken with the pope, Henry was reluctant – within clearly defined limits – to let theological differences alone rob him of servants he really liked, as long as they recognized him as Supreme Head of the Church. Cromwell benefited to a considerable degree from such flexibility until Henry felt that his chief minister had gone behind his back. But it is difficult to think of any truly selfless action that Henry performed; even those who seemingly enjoyed the security of his favour, such as Jane Seymour or Cranmer, would have been thrown to the wolves had it suited him.

Possessed of a deadly impatience in the face of knotty problems, from the moment he sent Empson and Dudley to their deaths at the beginning of his reign, Henry always looked for scapegoats when things went wrong. His vision of himself as Christ's deputy – and as the man who had proved to the world that the pope was 'only' the 'bishop of Rome' – could turn into a murderous paranoia. After Reginald Pole's relatives were beheaded, the French ambassador begged to be recalled, because 'he has to do with the most dangerous and cruel man in the world'.[52] No one, as Cromwell had once warned his Lutheran friends, knew for how long they would be safe.

Henry's rule was increasingly autocratic and his insistence on unquestioning obedience could verge on tyranny. 'You must beware,' a high-placed friend advised the Cambridge reformer Hugh Latimer when he first came to Court in 1530, 'that ye contrary not the king. Let him have his sayings; follow him; go with him.'[53] But although Henry behaved in ways that to modern eyes appear egoistical and arbitrary, he truly believed that his will was law. Once Foxe and Cranmer had convinced him that the King of England really was Christ's deputy, he believed he had a special relationship with God and saw himself as a patriarch as much as a king, hence the ease with which he became mesmerized by his own legend.

Despite this, his rule was never despotic. He was careful to use Parliament and the courts to legalize his break with Rome, and would never have thought of doing otherwise. True, he never expected Parliament or the judges to defy him, and individuals who opposed him were shown no mercy, but where he encountered more widespread discontent, he knew how to hold himself in check. During the crisis of the Pilgrimage of Grace, he instinctively knew when to pull back and turn to negotiations, even if he used false promises and crude psychological techniques to divide and cow the rebel leaders.

Thus, the suppression of the abbeys was approved by Parliament, the reports of informers in the 1530s were systematically sifted by Cromwell and criminal charges carefully weighed before prosecutions were begun. Most potential victims – with the exception, it must be said, of some of the friars and Carthusians – were tried by juries or convicted by act of Parliament. Henry shamelessly manipulated the law to suit his ends, while Cromwell rigged juries to ensure mistakes were avoided – for his own life depended on it. Otherwise, apart from those who defended the pope or were taken in open insurrection, few of his critics were ruined or destroyed. The vast majority were left in their positions – albeit closely watched. If people were prepared to accept (or at any rate, not deny in public) that the king was the Supreme Head of the Church, they were left to get on with their lives.

Of Henry's strengths, the most notable were his ability to

lead and inspire men, and his willingness to promote servants of low birth such as Wolsey and Cromwell to the highest positions because their talents deserved it. Of his character deficiencies, the greatest were his insatiable greed and invasive demands of allegiance. But for all his self-contradictions, Henry VIII was still the most remarkable ruler ever to sit on the English throne.

Notes

ABBREVIATIONS

AGS	Archivo General de Simancas
ASV	Archivum Secretum Vaticanum
Betteridge and Lipscomb	*Henry VIII and the Court: Art, Politics and Performance*, ed. T. Betteridge and S. Lipscomb (Farnham: Ashgate, 2013)
BL	British Library, London
BNF	Bibliothèque Nationale de France, Paris
Brown	*Four Years at the Court of Henry VIII: Selections of Despatches Written by the Venetian Ambassador, Sebastian Giustinian*, ed. R. Brown, 2 vols. (London: Smith, Elder, 1854)
Byrne	*The Letters of King Henry VIII*, ed. M. St Clare Byrne (London: Cassell, 1936)
CPR	*Calendar of Patent Rolls*, 69 vols. (London: 1891–1973)
CSP Milan	*State Papers and Manuscripts Existing in the Archives Collection of Milan*, ed. A. B. Hinds (London: 1913)
CSPSp	*Calendar of Letters, Despatches, and State Papers Relating to the Negotiations between England and Spain, Preserved in the Archives at Vienna, Brussels, Simancas and Elsewhere*, 13 vols. in 19 parts (London: 1862–1954)
CSPV	*Calendar of State Papers and Manuscripts Relating to English Affairs in the Archives and Collections of Venice and in Other Libraries of Northern Italy*, 38 vols. (London: 1864–1947)
Ellis	*Original Letters, Illustrative of British History*, ed. H. Ellis, 3 series, 11 vols. (London: Richard Bentley, 1824–46)
Foxe	John Foxe, *The first [and second] volume of the ecclesiasticall history contaynyng the actes and monumentes of thynges passed in euery kynges tyme in this realme, especially in the Church of England principally to be noted ... from the primitiue tyme till the reigne of K. Henry VIII*, 2 vols. (London: 1570)
Gunn and Lindley	*Cardinal Wolsey: Church, State and Art*, ed. S. J. Gunn and P. G. Lindley (Cambridge: Cambridge University Press, 1991)
Hall	*Henry VIII* (an edition of Edward Hall's *Chronicle*), ed. C. Whibley, 2 vols. (London: T. C. & E. C. Jack, 1904)
Hamilton Papers	*The Hamilton Papers. Letters and Papers Illustrating the Political Relations of England and Scotland in the 16th Century. Formerly in the Possession of the Dukes of Hamilton*, ed. J. Bain, 2 vols. (London: 1890–92)

Harpsfield	N. Harpsfield, *The Life and Death of Sir Thomas Moore, Knight, sometymes Lord High Chancellor of England, written in the tyme of Queene Marie*, ed. E. V. Hitchcock, Early English Text Society, Original Series, 186 (1932)
Herbert	Lord Herbert of Cherbury, *The Life and Reign of King Henry the Eighth* (London: M. Clark for Anne Mearne, 1682)
HJ	*Historical Journal*
HR	*Historical Research*
Inventory	*The Inventory of King Henry VIII*, ed. D. Starkey (London: Society of Antiquaries, 1998)
Ives	E. W. Ives, *The Life and Death of Anne Boleyn: 'The Most Happy'* (Oxford: Blackwell, 2004)
Knecht	R. Knecht, *Renaissance Warrior and Patron: The Reign of Francis I* (Cambridge: Cambridge University Press, 1994)
Lisle Letters	*The Lisle Letters*, ed. M. St Clare Byrne, 6 vols. (Chicago and London: University of Chicago Press, 1981)
LP	*Letters and Papers, Foreign and Domestic, of the Reign of Henry VIII*, ed. J. S. Brewer, J. Gairdner and R. H. Brodie, 21 vols. in 32 parts, and *Addenda* (London: 1862–1932)
McEntegart	R. McEntegart, *Henry VIII, The League of Schmalkalden and the English Reformation* (Woodbridge: Boydell & Brewer, 2002)
Merriman	*Life and Letters of Thomas Cromwell*, ed. R. B. Merriman, 2 vols. (Oxford: Clarendon Press, 1902)
More, SL	*St Thomas More: Selected Letters*, ed. E. F. Rogers (New Haven, Conn.: Yale University Press, 1961)
MS	Manuscript
NA	National Archives, Kew
PP Expenses	*The Privy Purse Expenses of King Henry the Eighth*, ed. N. H. Nicolas (London: William Pickering, 1827)
Scarisbrick	J. J. Scarisbrick, *Henry VIII* (London: Eyre & Spottiswoode, 1968)
Sicca and Waldman	*The Anglo-Florentine Renaissance: Art for the Early Tudors*, ed. C. M. Sicca and L. A. Waldman (New Haven, Conn., and London: Yale University Press, 2012)
State Papers	*State Papers During the Reign of Henry VIII*, Record Commission, 11 vols. (London: 1830–52)
TETL	*Two Early Tudor Lives*, ed. R. S. Sylvester and D. P. Harding (New Haven, Conn., and London: Yale University Press, 1962)
Vergil	*The Anglica Historia of Polydore Vergil, A.D. 1485–1537*, ed. D. Hay, Camden Society, 3rd Series, 74 (1950)
Vokes PhD	S. E. Vokes, 'The Early Career of Thomas Howard, Earl of Surrey and Third Duke of Norfolk, 1474–c.1525', unpublished Hull University PhD dissertation (1988)
Wriothesley	*A Chronicle of England during the Reigns of the Tudors, from A.D. 1485 to 1559, by Charles Wriothesley*, ed. W. D. Hamilton, 2 vols., Camden Society, New Series, 11 and 20 (1875–7)

Manuscripts preserved at the NA are quoted by the call number there in use. The descriptions of the classes referred to are as follows:

E 36	Exchequer, Treasury of the Receipt, Miscellaneous Books
E 154	Exchequer, King's Remembrancer and Treasury of the Receipt, Inventories of Goods and Chattels
KB 8	Court of King's Bench, Crown Side, Bag of Secrets
KB 9	Court of King's Bench, Ancient Indictments
LC 2	Lord Chamberlain's Department, Special Events
OBS	Obsolete Lists and Indexes
SP 1	State Papers, Henry VIII, General Series
SP 10	State Papers, Edward VI

INTRODUCTION

For the abbreviated titles used here, please see 'Abbreviations' on pp. 117–19.

1. NA, KB 8/7, Pt. 1 (*LP*, VIII, no. 609 (4)).
2. *CSPSp*, XII, p. 167.
3. T. Elyot, *Of the Knowledge whiche Maketh a Wise Man* (London: 1533), fos. 94–5.

I. SHAPING A LIFE

1. D. R. Starkey, *Henry: Virtuous Prince* (London: Harper Press, 2008), pp. 65–71. This pioneering study transforms our understanding of Henry's early life and I have relied heavily on it in this chapter.
2. *The Great Chronicle of London*, ed. A. H. Thomas and I. D. Thornley (Stroud: Alan Sutton, 1983), p. 252.
3. Folger Shakespeare Library, Washington, DC, PA6295.A3.1502 Cage. Compare Elizabeth of York's inscription of fourteen words and fifty-nine letters in a 1497 book of hours in the same library (facsimiles in *Folger's Choice*, ed. W. Gundersheimer (Washington, DC: Folger Shakespeare Library, 2008), items 8, 10).
4. *John Skelton: The Complete English Poems*, ed. J. Scattergood (London: Penguin, 1983), p. 132.
5. D. R. Carlson, 'Royal Tutors in the Reign of Henry VII', *Sixteenth Century Journal*, 22 (1991), pp. 265–6; *Collected Works of Erasmus*, ed. R. A. B. Mynors et al., 76 vols. (Toronto: University of Toronto Press, 1974–), I, pp. 195–7; *The Epistles of Erasmus*, ed. F. M. Nichols, 2 vols. (London: 1901), I, pp. 200–202; Starkey, *Henry: Virtuous Prince*, pp. 129–33.
6. *CPR, Henry VII, 1494–1509*, p. 72; Scarisbrick, p. 4.
7. *The Receyt of the Ladie Kateryne*, ed. G. Kipling, Early English Text Society, New Series, 296 (1990), pp. 12, 32, 36, 37, 42, 44, 49, 53, 55, 57–8.
8. *Receyt of the Ladie Kateryne*, pp. 78–9.
9. J. Guy, *The Children of Henry VIII* (Oxford: Oxford University Press, 2013), pp. 1–4.
10. *Receyt of the Ladie Kateryne*, p. 81.

11. *Opus Epistolarum Des. Erasmi Roterodami*, ed. P. S. Allen, 12 vols. (Oxford: Oxford University Press, 1906–58), I, p. 436; mistranslated in *Collected Works of Erasmus*, II, p. 129; Byrne, pp. 4–5.

12. NA, LC 2/1/1, fo. 73ᵛ.

13. Nicholas Orme, 'John Holt (d. 1504), Tudor Schoolmaster and Grammarian', *The Library*, 6th Series, 18 (1996), pp. 283–305; Carlson, 'Royal Tutors', pp. 270–73; *Collected Works of Erasmus*, II, pp. 128–9.

14. F. Bacon, *The Historie of the Raigne of King Henry the Seuenth* (London: 1622), p. 242.

15. *Correspondencia de Gutierre Gómez de Fuensalida*, ed. Duque de Berwick y de Alba (Madrid: Imprenta Alemana, 1907), p. 449.

16. *Letters and Papers Illustrative of the Reigns of Richard III and Henry VII*, ed. J. Gairdner, 2 vols. (London: 1861–3), I, p. 233.

17. *CSPSp*, I, no. 364.

18. *CSPSp*, I, nos. 325, 327, 354, 364, 370, 389, 396; Scarisbrick, pp. 9, 182–3.

19. *CSPSp*, I, no. 396; AGS, Patronato Real, leg. 53, doc. 92.

20. *LP*, I, ii, no. 2072. The best modern accounts of Philip's enforced visit are Starkey, *Henry: Virtuous Prince*, pp. 206–20; M. Biddle, *King Arthur's Round Table* (Woodbridge: Boydell Press, 2000), pp. 422–4.

21. Carlson, 'Royal Tutors', pp. 268, 276; D. R. Starkey, 'King Arthur and King Henry', in *Arthurian Literature, XVI*, ed. J. P. Carley and F. Riddy (Woodbridge: Boydell & Brewer, 1998), pp. 171–96. Prince Henry revealed his anti-French sentiment during the visit of Philip the Handsome to Windsor Castle, when a French diplomat suddenly arrived. See *Collection des voyages des souverains des Pays-Bas*, ed. M. Gachard, 4 vols. (Brussels: Hayez, 1876), I, pp. 425–6.

22. *Memorials of Henry VII*, ed. J. Gairdner (London: Longman, 1858), pp. 283–303; *Collection des voyages*, ed. Gachard, I, pp. 422–6; Biddle, *King Arthur's Round Table*, pp. 423–4; Starkey, *Henry: Virtuous Prince*, pp. 206–11.

23. *Collection des voyages*, ed. Gachard, I, p. 422.

24. *CSPSp*, IV, i, no. 224. I owe this reference to Julia Fox.

25. *Memorials of Henry VII*, ed. Gairdner, p. 116; Starkey, *Henry: Virtuous Prince*, pp. 227–9.

26. A. Young, *Tudor and Jacobean Tournaments* (London: George Philip, 1987), pp. 28–9.

27. *Memorials of Henry VII*, ed. Gairdner, pp. 120, 124.

28. *CSPSp*, I, no. 552.

29. C. J. Harrison, 'The Petition of Edmund Dudley', *English Historical Review*, 87 (1972), pp. 86–7. See also M. R. Horowitz, 'Policy and Prosecution in the Reign of Henry VII', *HR*, 82 (2009), pp. 412–58; M. R. Horowitz, ' "Agree with the King": Henry VII, Edmund Dudley and the Strange Case of Thomas Sunnyff', *HR*, 79 (2006), pp. 325–66.

30. M. K. Jones and M. G. Underwood, *The King's Mother: Lady Margaret Beaufort, Countess of Richmond and Derby* (Cambridge: Cambridge University Press, 1992), pp. 91–2, 235–6; M. M. Condon, 'The Last Will of Henry VII', in *Westminster Abbey: The Lady Chapel of Henry VII*, ed. T. W. T. Tatton-Brown and R. Mortimer (Woodbridge: Boydell Press, 2003), p. 105.

31. S. J. Gunn, 'The Accession of Henry VIII', *HR*, 64 (1991), pp. 278–88.

32. Condon, 'The Last Will of Henry VII', p. 103, n. 13; Gunn, 'Accession of Henry VIII', p. 283; J. Fisher, *This sermon folowynge was compyled [and] sayd in the cathedrall*

chyrche of saynt Poule . . . by the ryght reuerende fader in god Iohn bysshop of Roch-ester (London: 1509), sig. A3–[A4]. Fisher says that these conversations had begun 'at the beginning of Lent last past', i.e. 21 February 1509. I am grateful to David Starkey for directing me to this source.

33. Gunn, 'Accession of Henry VIII', p. 283; *Collected Works of Erasmus*, II, pp. 147–8.
34. H. Miller, *Henry VIII and the English Nobility* (Oxford: Blackwell, 1986), pp. 7–9.
35. *LP*, IV, iii, no. 5774 (6); Scarisbrick, pp. 12–13.
36. Byrne, pp. 9–11.
37. NA, KB 8/4.
38. AGS, Patronato Real, leg. 54, doc. 100; *CSPSp*, II, no. 19; Byrne, p. 11.
39. That Dudley in particular had useful information is proved by Harrison, 'Petition of Edmund Dudley', pp. 86–90, and NA, E 154/2/17, an inventory of his goods found at his house in Candlewick Street, London, which lists boxes of obligations and 'evidences' found in almost every room except the bedroom.
40. R. Rex, 'The Religion of Henry VIII', *HJ*, 57 (2014), p. 22.

2. THE POPE'S LOYAL SON

1. *CSPV*, II, no. 11; *LP*, I, i, nos. 153, 406.
2. *CSPV*, II, nos. 28, 33, 45; Vokes PhD, pp. 71–2.
3. *LP*, I, i, no. 842.
4. Vergil, pp. 160–62.
5. Ibid.; *CSPV*, II, no. 109.
6. Vergil, pp. 164–214; Vokes PhD, pp. 85–133; Scarisbrick, pp. 28–40.
7. A. Ferrajoli, 'Un breve inedito di Giulio II per la investitura del regno di Francia ad Enrico VIII d'Inghilterra', in *Archivio della Società Romana di Storia Patria*, 19 (1896), pp. 425–61; *LP*, I, ii, nos. 2527, 2688.
8. *TETL*, pp. 12–14.
9. Vergil, p. 246.
10. *LP*, I, ii, no. 3435; *CSPV*, II, no. 505.
11. *LP*, II, i, no. 894.
12. *CSPV*, II, no. 633; Brown, I, p. 103.
13. *CSPV*, III, nos. 18, 509.
14. Byrne, p. 28; *State Papers*, I, p. 1.
15. *LP*, II, i, p. cclxxxi.
16. *LP*, I, ii, nos. 2609, 2619, 2634, 2697, 2703; *CSPV*, II, nos. 382, 945.
17. *LP*, II, ii, no. 4009.
18. *CSPV*, II, no. 950.
19. *TETL*, p. 39; *State Papers*, VI, p. 334.
20. Byrne, p. 28.
21. *LP*, III, i, no. 950.
22. Brown, I, p. 155.
23. *CSPV*, III, no. 50; *LP*, III, i, nos. 869, 870, 871; S. Anglo, *Spectacle, Pageantry and Early Tudor Policy* (Oxford: Clarendon Press, 1969), pp. 124–69; G. Richardson, 'Personal Gift-giving at the Field of Cloth of Gold', in Betteridge and Lipscomb, pp. 48–9.
24. *CSPV*, III, no. 50

25. Ellis, 2nd Series, I, p. 177.

26. Brown, I, pp. 85–7.

27. *TETL*, p. 202.

28. George Puttenham, *The Arte of English Poesie* (London: 1589), p. 246.

29. Hall, I, p. 22.

30. *The Great Chronicle of London*, ed. A. H. Thomas and I. D. Thornley (Stroud: Alan Sutton, 1983), pp. 374–5.

31. C. B. Whiteley and K. Kramer, 'A New Explanation for the Reproductive Woes and Midlife Crisis of Henry VIII', *HJ*, 53 (2010), pp. 827–48.

32. *Records of the Reformation: The Divorce, 1527–1533*, ed. N. Pocock, 2 vols. (Oxford: Clarendon Press, 1870), II, p. 386.

33. Guy, *Children of Henry VIII*, pp. 20, 21, 37–9, 44, 63, 86, 89.

34. *CSPV*, II, no. 479; *LP*, I, ii, no. 3581.

35. NA, OBS 1419; *CSPV*, III, no. 167.

36. *LP*, II, i, no. 1581.

37. BL, Additional MS 19398, fo. 44.

38. NA, KB 9/441, no. 6; *LP*, III, i, nos. 1268, 1293.

39. NA, KB 9/53; NA, KB 8/5; BL, Harleian MS 283, fo. 72; *LP*, III, i, nos. 1284 (1–5), 1285 (pp. 495–505), 1356; *CSPV* III, no. 213.

40. *Yale Edition of the Complete Works of St Thomas More*, ed. L. L. Martz, R. S. Sylvester, C. H. Miller et al., 15 vols. (New Haven, Conn.: Yale University Press, 1963–97), I, pp. 128–82 (especially pp. 153–61).

41. Rex, 'Religion of Henry VIII', pp. 7–8; *LP*, III, i, no. 1293. Since at least the 1480s, the shrine had also been promoted at St George's Chapel, Windsor, which housed Schorne's relics. See *Proceedings of the Bury and West Suffolk Archaeological Institute*, 1 (1853), p. 222.

42. *LP*, II, ii, nos. 4257, 4266; *LP*, III, i, no. 1233; *CSPV*, III, nos. 210, 213.

43. *TETL*, p. 235.

44. Biblioteca Apostolica Vaticana, Membr.III.4; Nello Vian, 'La presentazione e gli esemplari Vaticani della *Assertio Septem Sacramentorum* di Enrico VIII', in *Collectanea Vaticana in Honorem M. Card. Anselmi Albareda a Biblioteca Apostolica edita*, Studi e Testi, 220 (1962), pp. 355–75; *LP*, III, ii, no. 1510.

45. *LP*, III, ii, 1659.

46. *LP*, III, i, no. 1369; *LP*, III, ii, nos. 1411, 1468, 1508, 1510, 1522, 1714, 1715; Herbert, pp. 102–44; W. E. Wilkie, *The Cardinal Protectors of England: Rome and the Tudors before the Reformation* (Cambridge: Cambridge University Press, 1974), pp. 122–5.

47. Anglo, *Spectacle, Pageantry*, pp. 170–206.

48. Herbert, pp. 142–4.

49. S. J. Gunn, 'The Duke of Suffolk's March on Paris in 1523', *English Historical Review*, 101 (1986), pp. 596–634.

50. Herbert, pp. 149–57; Knecht, pp. 208–18.

51. Knecht, pp. 218–27.

52. *CSPSp*, III, i, no. 33.

53. *State Papers*, VI, pp. 412–36; Herbert, pp. 157–9.

54. *LP*, IV, i, nos. 1440, 1443, 1474, 1487, 1493, 1525, 1531, 1557, 1563, 1578, 1589, 1617.

55. *State Papers*, I, pp. 153–6, 317–18; Byrne, pp. 76–80.

56. *State Papers*, VI, p. 421.

57. For an account of the proceedings, see *Inventories of the Wardrobes, Plate, Chapel*

Stuff etc. of Henry Fitzroy, Duke of Richmond, and of the Wardrobe Stuff at Baynard's Castle of Katherine, Princess Dowager, ed. J. Nichols, Camden Society, Old Series, 61 (1855), pp. lxxx–lxxxiv; *LP*, IV, i, no. 1431 (8); Hall, II, pp. 49–50.

58. *LP*, III, ii, p. 1539.
59. *LP*, III, ii, no. 3358.
60. *CSPV*, IV, no. 824.
61. *William Latymer's Chronickille of Anne Bulleyne*, ed. M. Dowling, Camden Miscellany, 4th Series, 30 (1990), p. 63.
62. *Letters of the Kings of England*, ed. J. O. Halliwell, 2 vols. (London: Henry Colburn, 1848), I, pp. 303–4.
63. Herbert, pp. 173–97; Knecht, pp. 239–60.
64. Herbert, pp. 209–10; J. Sharkey, 'The Politics of Wolsey's Cardinalate, 1515–1530', unpublished Cambridge University PhD dissertation (2008), pp. 166–7; S. J. Gunn, 'Wolsey's Foreign Policy and the Domestic Crisis of 1527–8', in Gunn and Lindley, pp. 151–2.
65. J. Sharkey, 'Between King and Pope: Thomas Wolsey and the Knight Mission', *HR*, 84 (2011), pp. 236–48.

3. A MAN OF CONSCIENCE

1. *CSPSp*, III, ii, no. 113.
2. More, *SL*, no. 53.
3. NA, SP 1/63, fos. 1–228ᵛ (a collection of fragments of the king's book); Trinity College, Cambridge, MS B.15.19 (a polished version of the book used as Henry's *libellus* at Blackfriars in 1529). The various 'King's books' or dossiers, iteratively compiled by Edward Foxe and his team, are described by *The Divorce Tracts of Henry VIII*, ed. E. Surtz and V. M. Murphy (Angers: Moreana, 1988), pp. i–xxxvi.
4. *Divorce Tracts*, ed. Surtz and Murphy, pp. xii–xiii; R. Rex, *The Theology of John Fisher* (Cambridge: Cambridge University Press, 1991), pp. 165–70.
5. More, *SL*, no. 53.
6. *Divorce Tracts*, ed. Surtz and Murphy, pp. xxviii–xxxvi, 167–85, 260–78.
7. *LP*, IV, ii, nos. 3363, 3400; Sharkey, 'Between King and Pope', pp. 247–8.
8. *LP*, IV, ii, no. 4858; J. Fox, *Sister Queens: Katherine of Aragon and Juana, Queen of Castile* (London: Weidenfeld & Nicolson, 2011), pp. 289–91.
9. NA, PRO 31/9/4 (Stevenson's nineteenth-century transcripts of documents from the Vatican Archives, shelfmark then said to be ASV, 4/209).
10. C. Fletcher, *Our Man in Rome: Henry VIII and his Italian Ambassador* (London: Bodley Head, 2012), pp. 81–8, 96–7.
11. *TETL*, pp. 95–100.
12. *TETL*, p. 101.
13. Herbert, pp. 302–3.
14. Herbert, pp. 339–43; *TETL*, pp. 101–93.
15. More, *SL*, p. 209.
16. Guy, *Children of Henry VIII*, p. 73.
17. *Narratives of the Days of the Reformation*, ed. J. G. Nicholls, Camden Society, 1st Series, 77 (1859), pp. 52–7.
18. BL, Cotton MS, Cleopatra E.VI, fos. 16–135; G. D. Nicholson, 'The Act of Appeals

and the English Reformation', in *Law and Government under the Tudors*, ed. Claire Cross, D. M. Loades and J. J. Scarisbrick (Cambridge: Cambridge University Press, 1988), pp. 19–30.

19. J. Guy, 'Thomas Cromwell and the Intellectual Origins of the Henrician Revolution', in *The Tudor Monarchy*, ed. J. Guy (London: Arnold, 1997), pp. 213–33.

20. J. Guy, 'Henry VIII and the *Praemunire* Manoeuvres of 1530–1531', *English Historical Review*, 97 (1982), pp. 481–503.

21. J. Guy, *The Public Career of Sir Thomas More* (New Haven, Conn.: Yale University Press, 1980), pp. 113–201.

22. Herbert, pp. 366–9; Hall, II, pp. 218–21; CSPV, IV, no. 824; LP, V, nos. 1373–4, 1484–5, 1492; *The maner of the tryumphe at Caleys [and] Bulleyn. The second pryntyng, with mo[re] addicio[n]s as it was done in dede* (London: 1532).

23. CSPV, IV, no. 824.

24. D. MacCulloch, *Thomas Cranmer: A Life* (New Haven, Conn., and London: Yale University Press, 1996), pp. 637–8.

25. Knecht, pp. 298–9; Ives, pp. 161–4.

26. LP, VI, nos. 230, 254; Knecht, pp. 298–9.

27. Byrne, pp. 120–21; *State Papers*, VII, pp. 427–37; LP, VI, no. 230.

28. LP, V, no. 1292.

29. Noted on an early draft of the Act of Appeals: BL, Cotton MS, Cleopatra E.VI, fos. 180–84.

30. LP, VI, nos. 561, 563, 564, 583, 584, 601, 602; Hall, II, pp. 229–42; Ives, pp. 173–83.

31. LP, VI, no. 585.

32. Herbert, pp. 386–7; LP, VI, nos. 954, 1038, 1042.

33. Herbert, p. 387; LP, VI, 1425–7; Knecht, pp. 301–2.

34. LP, VI, no. 1404.

35. LP, VI, nos. 923, 1503; LP, VIII, nos. 196, 278, 809.

36. More, *SL*, nos. 47, 50, 51, 53 (p. 206), 54 (p. 222); LP, VI, nos. 1419, 1464, 1465, 1466, 1519, 1546; LP, VII, no. 522.

37. More, *SL*, nos. 50, 51, 52, 53; LP, VII, nos. 48, 52, 107, 238, 239, 240.

38. Herbert, pp. 397, 401; LP, VII, nos. 362–4.

39. S. Lehmberg, *The Reformation Parliament 1529–1536* (Cambridge: Cambridge University Press, 1970), pp. 197–9.

40. Herbert, p. 408; LP, VII, nos. 590, 650, 807, 841, 856, 939, 953, 977, 1020, 1057, 1090, 1095, 1307, 1488, 1607; *Lisle Letters*, II, p. 130; G. R. Elton, *Policy and Police: The Enforcement of the Reformation in the Age of Thomas Cromwell* (Cambridge: Cambridge University Press, 1972), pp. 222–7; D. Knowles, *The Religious Orders in England*, 3 vols. (Cambridge: Cambridge University Press, 1948–59), III, pp. 202–10, 379–82.

41. Herbert, pp. 415–18.

42. S. G. Ellis, *Tudor Frontiers and Noble Power: The Making of the British State* (Oxford: Oxford University Press, 1995), pp. 209–32.

43. 26 Hen.VIII, c. 13; for an account of the proceedings in Parliament, see Lehmberg, *Reformation Parliament*, pp. 204–6.

44. NA, KB 8/7, Pt. 1.

45. LP, VIII, nos. 565, 567, 609, 661, 666; Guildhall Library, London, MS 1231; NA, KB 8/7, Pt. 1; CSPMilan, I, no. 965; CSPSp, V, i, no. 156; P. Hughes, *The Reformation in England*, 3 vols. (London: Hollis & Carter, 1950), I, pp. 279–80; J. Guy, *A Daughter's Love: Thomas and Margaret More* (London: 4th Estate, 2008), p. 253.

46. *LP*, VIII, no. 742.
47. F. Van Ortroy, 'Vie du Bienheureux Martyr Jean Fisher, Cardinal', *Analecta Bollandiana*, 10 (1891), pp. 161, 170–88; NA, KB 8/7, Pt. 2; Harpsfield, pp. 232–4, 236–41.
48. NA, KB 8/7, Pt. 3; BNF, MS FF 1701 (fos. 185–90), 2832 (fos. 191–3), 2960 (fos. 64–70), 2981 (fos. 44–5), 3969 (fos. 63–7), 12795 (fos. 29–32), 16539 (fos. 30–33); Harpsfield, pp. 258–66; ASV, Archivum Arcis, Arm I–XVIII, MS 3265 (my thanks to Jessica Sharkey for this reference and a photocopy); *TETL*, pp. 244–50; J. D. M. Derrett, 'Neglected Versions of the Contemporary Account of the Trial of Sir Thomas More', *Bulletin of the Institute of Historical Research*, 33 (1960), pp. 202–23.
49. Guy, *A Daughter's Love*, pp. 250–51, 258–9, 324.
50. *LP*, IX, no. 226; *LP*, V, no. 221, establishes Coverdale's links to Cromwell.
51. A. Freeman, 'To Guard His Words', *The Times Literary Supplement*, issue 5463 (14 December 2007), pp. 13–14.
52. Herbert, pp. 410–12; *CSPSp*, V, i, no. 170.
53. *LP*, VII, nos. 1257, 1554.
54. *LP*, VIII, no. 263; *Lisle Letters*, V, no. 1086; S. Brigden, *Thomas Wyatt: The Heart's Forest* (London: Faber and Faber, 2012), pp. 191–5.
55. *LP*, IX, no. 571; *William Latymer's Chronickille*, ed. Dowling, p. 62.
56. *LP*, X, no. 901; J. Fox, *Jane Boleyn: The Infamous Lady Rochford* (London: Weidenfeld & Nicolson, 2007), pp. 180–81.
57. *LP*, X, no. 141; Hall, II, p. 266.
58. *CSPSp*, V, ii, no. 21.
59. Hall, I, pp. 319–20; II, p. 38.
60. Wriothesley, I, p. 33; *LP*, X, nos. 200, 294; *LP*, XII, ii, no. 77; *LP*, XIII, ii, nos. 804 (5), 979 (7); *CSPSp*, V, ii, no. 35; NA, KB 8/11, Pt. 2, m. 7.
61. *CSPSp*, V, ii, no. 29.
62. *LP*, X, no. 199.
63. *CSPSp*, V, ii, no. 43; *LP*, X, no. 615; Ives, pp. 308–9.
64. *Annals of the Reformation and Establishment of Religion*, ed. J. Strype, 3 vols. in 7 parts (Oxford: Clarendon Press, 1725–7), I, p. 433.
65. NA, KB 8/8–9; *LP*, X, nos. 782, 784–5, 798, 838, 876, 908; Hall, II, pp. 268–9; Wriothesley, I, pp. 189–226; Ives, pp. 319–56.
66. *LP*, X, nos. 848, 876.
67. Ibid., no. 908.
68. Ibid., no. 1000.
69. 28 Hen. VIII, c. 7.
70. *LP*, X, nos. 977, 1077; Herbert, p. 451.

4. ARBITER OF CHRISTENDOM

1. *CSPSp*, V, ii, no. 9; *LP*, X, nos. 1108, 1110, and pp. xxxvii–xxxviii; *LP*, XI, no. 7; Herbert, p. 450.
2. *LP*, X, nos. 1110, 1137; *LP*, XI, no. 7.
3. *LP*, X, no. 975; E. Duffy, 'Hampton Court, Henry VIII and Cardinal Pole', in Betteridge and Lipscomb, pp. 203–6.
4. *LP*, XI, nos. 531, 536, 705, 761, 841, 892, 902, 968, 971–5, 1080, 1086, 1155, 1182; *State Papers*, I, pp. 463–6, 468–70, 473–8, 485–7, 491–510.

5. *LP*, XI, nos. 860, 1250.

6. *LP*, XI, nos. 1227, 1235, 1244, 1246; *State Papers*, I, pp. 511–23.

7. *State Papers*, I, pp. 523–4; *Lisle Letters*, IV, no. 910.

8. *LP*, XII, i, nos. 67, 138, 146, 147, 163, 200, 201, 202.

9. *State Papers*, I, pp. 538–9.

10. *Miscellaneous Writings and Letters of Thomas Cranmer*, ed. J. E. Cox (London: Parker Society, 1846), p. 105.

11. *LP*, XII, i, no. 779.

12. *LP*, XII, i, nos. 1032, 1235, 1242; *LP*, XIII, ii, no. 766; Brigden, *Thomas Wyatt*, pp. 329–32.

13. McEntegart, pp. 26–58.

14. *LP*, X, no. 1085.

15. McEntegart, p. 45.

16. He maintained until his death that he could achieve this. See *The Letters of Stephen Gardiner*, ed. J. A. Muller (Cambridge: Cambridge University Press, 1933), p. 301.

17. *LP*, XI, nos. 59, 123, 377, 954, 1110; Merriman, II, no. 159.

18. *The institution of a Christen man conteynynge the exposytion or interpretation of the commune Crede [&c.]* (London: 1537); MacCulloch, *Thomas Cranmer*, pp. 185–94.

19. Ellis, III, iii, pp. 196–7; *LP*, XII, i, no. 790; J. Guy, *Christopher St German on Chancery and Statute*, Selden Society, Supplementary Series, 6 (1985), pp. 46–7.

20. *A Protestation made for the Most Mighty and Most Redoubted King of England* (London: 1538), sig. C4ᵛ–5; Rex, 'Religion of Henry VIII', p. 30; T. Sowerby, *Renaissance and Reform in Tudor England: The Careers of Sir Richard Morison, c.1513–1556* (Oxford: Oxford University Press, 2010), pp. 67–9.

21. *A Necessary doctrine and erudition for any Christen man set furthe by the Kynges Maiestie of Englande &c.* (London: 1543).

22. A. Ryrie, *The Gospel and Henry VIII* (Cambridge: Cambridge University Press, 2003), pp. 13–39.

23. 31 Hen. VIII, c. 14.

24. BL, Cotton MS, Cleopatra E.IV, fos. 131–3; *Miscellaneous Writings and Letters*, ed. Cox, pp. 96–100; Scarisbrick, pp. 384–423; G. W. Bernard, 'The Making of Religious Policy, 1533–46: Henry VIII and the Search for the Middle Way', *HJ*, 41 (1998), pp. 321–49.

25. MacCulloch, *Thomas Cranmer*, pp. 196–7.

26. BL, Cotton MS, Cleopatra E.IV, fo. 348.

27. *LP*, XII, ii, no. 971.

28. *LP*, XII, ii, no. 972.

29. Knecht, pp. 334–41, 385–9.

30. McEntegart, p. 87; Herbert, p. 493.

31. McEntegart, pp. 98–9.

32. *The institution of a Christen man*, fos. 70–72, 119ᵛ–20; *Miscellaneous Writings and Letters*, ed. Cox, pp. 100–101; MacCulloch, *Thomas Cranmer*, pp. 214–15, 226–7; Merriman, II, no. 273.

33. *LP*, XIII, ii, no. 303; T. F. Mayer, 'Becket's Bones Burnt! Cardinal Pole and the Invention and Dissemination of an Atrocity', in *Martyrs and Martyrdom in England, c.1400–1700*, ed. T. S. Freeman and T. F. Mayer (Woodbridge: Boydell Press, 2007), pp. 126–43.

34. Knowles, *Religious Orders in England*, III, pp. 350–92; Herbert, pp. 504–5.

35. McEntegart, p. 132; Herbert, p. 493.

36. *LP*, XIII, ii, nos. 849, 851, 899; McEntegart, pp. 133–4; MacCulloch, *Thomas Cranmer*, pp. 232–4.
37. *Lisle Letters*, V, pp. 291–3; Hall, II, p. 283; Herbert, p. 501.
38. Byrne, pp. 232–4.
39. *Lisle Letters*, V, pp. 284–5; Herbert, pp. 501–2; T. Sowerby, 'Richard Pate, the Royal Supremacy and Reformation Diplomacy', *HJ*, 54 (2011), pp. 265–85; H. Pierce, *Margaret Pole, Countess of Salisbury, 1473–1531* (Cardiff: University of Wales Press, 2003), pp. 173–7.
40. *LP*, XIII, ii, nos. 1087, 1088; Herbert, p. 501.
41. Duffy, 'Hampton Court, Henry VIII and Cardinal Pole', pp. 231–2; Herbert, p. 505.
42. *LP*, XIII, i, nos. 123, 191, 329, 338, 756, 1126, 1132, 1133, 1198; *LP*, XIV, ii, no. 400; Herbert, pp. 496–7; Scarisbrick, pp. 356–8.
43. *LP*, XIII, i, nos. 1355, 1403, 1451, 1496; *LP*, XIII, ii, nos. 77, 232, 277; Scarisbrick, pp. 358–60.
44. *LP*, XIV, i, no. 920.
45. McEntegart, pp. 141–4; Bernard, 'The Making of Religious Policy, 1533–46', pp. 344–5.
46. *LP*, XV, nos. 23, 822, 823, 850; Herbert, pp. 515–16; Hall, II, pp. 294–303; Scarisbrick, pp. 370–71.
47. *LP*, XV, no. 823.
48. A. J. Slavin, 'Cromwell, Lisle and the Calais Sacramentarians: The Politics of Conspiracy', *Albion*, 9 (1977), pp. 316–36.
49. McEntegart, p. 134, n. 13.
50. One of Cromwell's trusted servants, Bartholomew Traheron, had travelled to Switzerland, met Heinrich Bullinger and then invited Swiss scholars back to England. See *Original Letters Relative to the English Reformation . . . Chiefly from the Archives of Zurich*, ed. H. Robinson, 2 vols. (Cambridge: Parker Society, 1846–7), I, no. 149 (for the correct date of this letter, January 1538, see MacCulloch, *Thomas Cranmer*, p. 184); II, nos. 279, 283, 287; MacCulloch, *Thomas Cranmer*, pp. 176–7, 184–5; Mary Robertson, 'Thomas Cromwell's Servants', unpublished UCLA PhD dissertation (1975), pp. 574–5.
51. McEntegart, pp. 199–200; Herbert, pp. 515–16, 518–19; *LP*, XV, nos. 821, 822, 823, 824, 938.
52. G. R. Elton, 'Thomas Cromwell's Decline and Fall', *Cambridge Historical Journal*, 10 (1951), pp. 150–85.
53. Herbert, pp. 532–6; Fox, *Jane Boleyn*, pp. 291–303.
54. Herbert, pp. 525–6, 529–30; Knecht, pp. 393–7.
55. *LP*, XVII, no. 523; Byrne, p. 356.
56. Byrne, p. 356.
57. Knecht, pp. 478–80.
58. Herbert, pp. 530–31; *Hamilton Papers*, I, no. 22; Byrne, pp. 282–4, 292–303.
59. Herbert, pp. 542–5.
60. Byrne, pp. 303–4; Hall, II, pp. 339–40.
61. Herbert, pp. 547–8; Hall, II, pp. 340–41; Byrne, pp. 311–27.
62. *LP*, XVIII, i, nos. 804, 805.
63. Herbert, pp. 548–51; Byrne, pp. 327–37.
64. *LP*, XIX, i, nos. 387, 389, 404, 405, 411, 416, 432, 472, 483; Byrne, pp. 346–7; Herbert, pp. 569–70.
65. Herbert, p. 541.
66. Herbert, pp. 553–7.

67. G. Richardson, 'Hunting at the Courts of Francis I and Henry VIII', *The Court Historian*, 18 (2013), pp. 132–3.
68. E. T. Hurren, 'Cultures of the Body, Medical Regimen and Physic at the Tudor Court', in Betteridge and Lipscomb, p. 67. Those measurements probably overestimated his physical bulk by a few inches as his body had to fit inside the steel.
69. *LP*, XIII, i, no. 995; *CSPSp*, VII, nos. 56, 99, 100; *LP*, XIX, i, no. 263.
70. *CSPSp*, VII, no. 99.
71. *LP*, XVIII, i, nos. 873, 875.
72. *Katherine Parr: Complete Works and Correspondence*, ed. J. Mueller (Chicago: University of Chicago Press, 2011), p. 621.
73. Byrne, pp. 367–8.
74. Herbert, pp. 575–6.
75. *CSPSp*, VII, no. 124.
76. Herbert, p. 577; Byrne, p. 368.
77. *LP*, XVIII, i, nos. 144, 339; Herbert, pp. 554–5, 578–82.
78. Byrne, pp. 371–417.
79. *LP*, XX, i, nos. 301, 303, 311–13, 1263; Herbert, pp. 586–9; M. Rule, 'The Sinking of the *Mary Rose*', *History Today*, 32 (1982), pp. 27–36.
80. *LP*, XXI, i, nos. 469, 550, 551, 582, 588, 1463, 1526; Herbert, pp. 609–11.
81. *State Papers*, X, pp. 134–6; Byrne, pp. 379–87, 395–417.
82. T. Mayer, *Reginald Pole: Prince and Prophet* (Cambridge: Cambridge University Press, 2000), pp. 143–63.

5. A SECOND SOLOMON

1. Hall, I, p. 15; *LP*, X, no. 141.
2. M. Hayward, *Dress at the Court of Henry VIII* (Leeds: Maney, 2007), pp. 95–128, 321–2.
3. Hall, II, pp. 85–8; *CSPV*, IV, no. 105. See also *CSPV*, II, no. 918.
4. *Inventory, passim*; *PP Expenses*, pp. 43, 108.
5. Biddle, *King Arthur's Round Table*, pp. 432–45.
6. S. Thurley, 'The Domestic Building Works of Cardinal Wolsey', in Gunn and Lindley, pp. 76–102.
7. S. Thurley, *The Royal Palaces of Tudor England* (New Haven, Conn., and London: Yale University Press, 1993), pp. 39–48; Westminster Abbey Muniments, MS 63,509.
8. R. Illingworth, 'Transcript of a Draft of an Indenture of Covenants for the Erecting of a Tomb to the Memory of King Henry the Eighth, and Queen Katherine his Wife', *Archaeologia*, 16 (1812), pp. 84–8.
9. G. Gentilini and T. Mozzati, '"Life-size Figures … with the King on Horseback": Baccio Bandinelli's Mausoleum for Henry VIII', in Sicca and Waldman, pp. 203–25.
10. A. Higgins, 'On the Work of Florentine Sculptors in England in the Early Part of the Sixteenth Century', *Archaeological Journal*, 51 (1894), pp. 164–91; P. G. Lindley, 'Playing Check-Mate with Royal Majesty? Wolsey's Patronage of Italian Renaissance Sculpture', in Gunn and Lindley, pp. 267–8.
11. T. P. Campbell, *Henry VIII and the Art of Majesty* (New Haven, Conn., and London: Yale University Press, 2007), pp. 127–67.
12. Ibid., pp. 114–25, 169–79.

13. *Receyt of the Ladie Kateryne*, pp. 72–3; *Inventory*, nos. 15, 364–419.

14. *LP*, III, i, nos. 1285, 1286; NA, E 36/171 (a partial inventory of Wolsey's goods); Campbell, *Henry VIII and the Art of Majesty*, pp. 167–9, 201–3.

15. S. Foister, *Holbein and England* (New Haven, Conn., and London: Yale University Press, 2004), pp. 9, 11, 24, 46, 54–5, 59, 75, 77, 117, 123, 232–3, 247–52; J. Rowlands, *Holbein: The Paintings of Hans Holbein the Younger* (London: Phaidon, 1985), pp. 69–72, 132–3, 222–3.

16. Foister, *Holbein and England*, pp. 159–65.

17. *Lost Faces: Identity and Discovery in Tudor Royal Portraiture*, ed. D. Starkey and B. Grosvenor (London: Philip Mould, 2007), pp. 4–7.

18. S. Thurley, *Whitehall Palace: An Architectural History of the Royal Apartments, 1240–1690* (New Haven, Conn., and London: Yale University Press, 1999), pp. 48–9, 64.

19. Foister, *Holbein and England*, pp. 175–96; Rowlands, *Holbein*, pp. 224–6 and plates 195–9; T. String, 'Henry VIII and Holbein: Patterns and Conventions in Early Modern Writing about Artists', in Betteridge and Lipscomb, pp. 134–6.

20. Rowlands, *Holbein*, pp. 224–5.

21. Foister, *Holbein and England*, pp. 152–5; Rowlands, *Holbein*, pp. 91–3, 150. In a place where Holbein's first inscription differed slightly from the usual text of the Vulgate, the word 'constitutus' (the meaning of which could be ambiguous) was bracketed by someone to remove any suggestion that Henry had been 'elected' king by popular consent rather than 'established' by God.

22. *Hans Holbein the Younger: Portraitist of the Renaissance*, ed. A. van Suchtelen, Q. Buvelot and P. van der Ploeg (The Hague: Waanders, 2003), no. 33.

23. Foister, *Holbein and England*, pp. 196–8; Rowlands, *Holbein*, pp. 146–7 and colour plate 32.

24. S. Foister, *Holbein in England* (London: Tate Britain, 2006), p. 100.

25. BL, Royal MS, 2 A.XVI.

26. Campbell, *Henry VIII and the Art of Majesty*, pp. 261–75.

27. Ibid., pp. 281–97.

28. Ibid., p. 282.

29. Thurley, *Royal Palaces*, pp. 60–65; M. Biddle, 'Nonsuch, Henry VIII's Mirror for a Prince', in Sicca and Waldman, pp. 307–44.

30. Biddle, 'Nonsuch, Henry VIII's Mirror for a Prince', pp. 336–43.

31. Sir Thomas Elyot, *The Book Named the Governor*, ed. S. E. Lehmberg (London: Dent, 1962), p. 37; L. Jardine, *Erasmus, Man of Letters: The Construction of Charisma in Print* (Princeton: Princeton University Press, 1993), pp. 30–39.

32. *LP*, XIII, ii, no. 77.

6. EPILOGUE

1. *LP*, XIII, i, no. 995.

2. *LP*, XIX, i, no. 529; *CSPSp*, VII, no. 99.

3. Hayward, *Dress at the Court of Henry VIII*, pp. 117–18; *The 1542 Inventory of Whitehall: The Palace and its Keeper*, ed. M. Hayward, 2 vols. (London: Illuminata Publishers for the Society of Antiquaries of London, 2004), I, p. 37.

4. *The 1542 Inventory*, ed. Hayward, II, no. 3676.

5. *LP*, XXI, ii, no. 642.

6. *The 1542 Inventory*, ed. Hayward, II, nos. 3677, 3680.

7. *LP*, XXI, ii, no. 238; Herbert, p. 625.

8. Richardson, 'Hunting at the Courts of Francis I and Henry VIII', pp. 132–3.

9. Whiteley and Kramer, 'A New Explanation for the Reproductive Woes and Midlife Crisis of Henry VIII', pp. 837–48.

10. Henry E. Huntington Library, San Marino, California, MS HM 41955, fos. 113–16; *LP*, XIV, ii, no. 153.

11. *LP*, XXI, ii, no. 768.

12. *LP*, XXI, i, no. 1227.

13. *LP*, XVI, no. 589.

14. Brigden, *Thomas Wyatt*, pp. 465–92.

15. *LP*, XX, ii, no. 738.

16. *State Papers*, X, pp. 730–33.

17. S. E. James, *Kateryn Parr: The Making of a Queen* (Aldershot: Ashgate, 1999), pp. 22–39, 189–220.

18. 34 & 35 Hen. VIII, c. 1.

19. Ibid.

20. Foxe, pp. 1422–5; T. S. Freeman, 'One Survived: The Account of Katherine Parr in Foxe's *Book of Martyrs*', in Betteridge and Lipscomb, pp. 235–52; James, *Kateryn Parr*, pp. 274–80.

21. Freeman, 'One Survived', p. 236.

22. Foxe, pp. 1424–5; Freeman, 'One Survived', p. 237; James, *Kateryn Parr*, pp. 278–80.

23. 35 Hen. VIII, c. 1.

24. *Foedera, Conventiones, Litterae et Cuiuscunque Generis Acta Publica inter Reges Angliae et Alios Quosuis Imperatores, Reges, Pontifices, Principes vel Communitates*, ed. T. Rymer, 20 vols. (London: 1726–35), XV, pp. 110–17. The commonly received opinion that Henry decided specifically to exclude his great-niece Mary, Queen of Scots, from the succession is mistaken. Furious with the Scots for refusing to ratify the Treaty of Greenwich and for the humiliation they had inflicted on him at Ancrum Moor, he declined to mention either her or his niece Margaret Douglas (his elder sister's daughter by her second husband, the Earl of Angus). But legally, each was still entitled to stake her claim, if all else failed, as 'the next rightful heir'.

25. E. W. Ives, 'Henry VIII's Will: A Forensic Conundrum', *HJ*, 35 (1992), pp. 801–2.

26. *LP*, XXI, ii, no. 606; Ives, 'Henry VIII's Will', p. 783.

27. W. A. Sessions, *Henry Howard, the Poet Earl of Surrey: A Life* (Oxford: Clarendon Press, 1999), pp. 358–61; Herbert, pp. 623–31.

28. *LP*, XXI, ii, no. 555 (1–18).

29. *LP*, XXI, ii, no. 697.

30. Sessions, *Henry Howard*, pp. 369–72.

31. *LP*, XXI, ii, no. 605.

32. *LP*, XXI, ii, nos. 555 (14), 605, 606; Sessions, *Henry Howard*, pp. 368–9; S. Brigden, 'Henry Howard, Earl of Surrey, and the "Conjured League"', *HJ*, 37 (1994), pp. 507–37.

33. *LP*, XXI, ii, nos. 696, 753.

34. Foxe, p. 1477.

35. NA, SP 10/8, no. 4. I am grateful to Alan Bryson for discussing with me who exactly was present at Henry's bedside when he died.

36. *LP*, XXI, ii, no. 684.

37. The message now survives on a scrap of paper pasted inside the cover of Katherine Parr's book of psalms and prayers: *Katherine Parr*, ed. Mueller, p. 626.

38. *CSPSp*, IX, pp. 6–7.

39. I am grateful to Alan Bryson for clarification of the sequence of events.

40. *LP*, XXI, ii, no. 605; Ives, 'Henry VIII's Will', pp. 802–4.

41. *Journals of the House of Lords*, 61 vols. (London: 1767–), I, p. 291; *LP*, XXI, ii, nos. 760, 761; A. Bryson, '"The Special Men in Every Shire": The Edwardian Regime, 1547–1553', unpublished University of St Andrews PhD dissertation (2001), p. 30.

42. The candlesticks are at the Cathedral of St Bavo, Ghent; two candle-bearing angels were until recently at Great Harrowden Hall, Northamptonshire, where they had stood for many years above the posts of the entrance gates, and two more from the same source were sold at Sotheby's in 1994. See F. Caglioti, 'Benedetto da Rovezzano in England', in Sicca and Waldman, pp. 177–97. Two of these candlesticks were on display in June 2014 at the Victoria and Albert Museum, where they were the subject of a £5 million appeal to save them for the nation.

43. Higgins, 'On the Work of Florentine Sculptors in England', pp. 164–91; Lindley, 'Playing Check-Mate with Royal Majesty?', in Gunn and Lindley, pp. 267–8.

44. Duffy, 'Hampton Court, Henry VIII and Cardinal Pole', in Betteridge and Lipscomb, p. 198.

45. H. Halford, *An Account of What Appeared on Opening the Coffin of King Charles I in the Vault of King Henry the Eighth in St George's Chapel at Windsor* (London: John Murray, 1813), p. 10.

46. *Miscellaneous Writings and Letters*, ed. Cox, p. 117.

47. *Henry VIII: A European Court in England*, ed. D. R. Starkey (London: Collins & Brown, 1991), pp. 8–10.

48. *Inventory*, p. x.

49. J. P. Carley, *The Books of King Henry VIII and his Wives* (London: Collins & Brown, 2004), pp. 101–3.

50. S. E. Lehmberg, *The Later Parliaments of Henry VIII, 1536–1547* (Cambridge: Cambridge University Press, 1977), pp. 229–31.

51. Byrne, p. 128.

52. *LP*, XIV, i, no. 144.

53. *The Works of Hugh Latimer*, ed. G. E. Corrie, 2 vols. (Cambridge: Parker Society, 1844–5), I, p. 231.

Further Reading

The classic life of Henry VIII is still J. J. Scarisbrick's *Henry VIII* (London: Eyre & Spottiswoode, 1968). Written with rare narrative flair and beautifully paced, the book is especially rewarding for its shrewd insights into the king's mindset. Very little in it needs significant revision after almost fifty years. Readers interested in the king's first divorce suit should also consult V. Murphy, 'The Literature and Propaganda of Henry VIII's First Divorce', in *The Reign of Henry VIII: Politics, Policy and Piety*, ed. D. MacCulloch (Basingstoke: Macmillan, 1995), pp. 135–58, while those intrigued by Henry's Lutheran flirtations in the 1530s should refer to R. McEntegart, *Henry VIII, the League of Schmalkalden and the English Reformation* (Woodbridge: Boydell & Brewer, 2002).

Although not strictly a biography, D. R. Starkey's monumental *Six Wives: The Queens of Henry VIII* (London: Chatto & Windus, 2003) stands out as the most candid and discriminating account of Henry's relationship with his wives and courtiers, enlivened throughout by the author's puckish wit. For readers seeking something bite-sized, a compelling brief life is E. W. Ives, *Henry VIII* (Oxford: Oxford University Press, 2007), reprinted from his article in *Oxford Dictionary of National Biography* (Oxford: Oxford University Press, 2004), online edition http://www.oxforddnb.com/view/article/12955.

Beyond these standard works, L. B. Smith's *Henry VIII: The Mask of Royalty* (London: Cape, 1971) attempts a psychological profile of the king with mixed success, but the author's view of the last years of the reign is interesting. L. Wooding's *Henry VIII* (London: Routledge, 2009) is an enviable work of synthesis; a biographical study that also encompasses the chief historical themes transcending the reign, it is aimed mainly at students, who will be eternally grateful for the author's sober, careful scholarship and useful subheadings.

A landmark foray into Henry's childhood and early life, crammed with insights into the influence of both his parents, Henry VII and Elizabeth of York, is D. R. Starkey, *Henry: Virtuous Prince* (London: Harper Press, 2008). Of the many individual studies of the king's wives, a judicious recent account of Katherine of Aragon is J. Fox, *Sister Queens: Katherine of Aragon and Juana, Queen of Castile* (London: Weidenfeld & Nicolson, 2011), which, as the title suggests, is a double biography of Katherine and her sister Juana. E. W. Ives's *The Life and Death of Anne Boleyn: 'The Most Happy'* (Oxford: Blackwell, 2004) is a superbly researched biography of the woman who was the love of Henry VIII's life until things turned sour, and whose effect on him changed the face of England and the monarchy for ever. Jane Seymour's brief queenship has not yet justified a serious biography, but R. M. Warnicke's *The Marrying of Anne of Cleves* (Cambridge: Cambridge University Press, 2000) makes a good shot at Henry's brief encounter with his fourth wife.

An excellent investigation of the fall of Katherine Howard, based on an impressive deciphering of the almost illegible legal depositions in the case, can be found in J. Fox, *Jane Boleyn: The Infamous Lady Rochford* (London: Weidenfeld & Nicolson, 2007), a book which also includes important new material relevant to the fall of Anne Boleyn. An outstanding life of Katherine Parr is S. E. James's *Kateryn Parr: The Making of a Queen* (Aldershot: Ashgate, 1999), reissued in an abridged text as *Catherine Parr: Henry VIII's Last Love* (Stroud: Tempus, 2008).

Informative, easily accessible studies of the upbringing and adolescence of Henry's four children (the fourth being the illegitimate Henry Fitzroy) are J. Guy's *The Children of Henry VIII* (Oxford: Oxford University Press, 2013) – which takes note in passing of all of Henry's proven mistresses – B. A. Murphy's *Bastard Prince: Henry VIII's Lost Son* (Stroud: Sutton Publishing, 2001) and D. R. Starkey's *Elizabeth: Apprenticeship* (London: Chatto & Windus, 2000). Starkey's *Elizabeth*, linked to his Channel 4 television series, vividly rediscovers the early life of the last Tudor monarch up to the point of her coronation.

In his biography of Anne Boleyn and in several scholarly articles, e.g. 'Faction at the Court of Henry VIII: The Fall of Anne Boleyn', *History*, 57 (1972), pp. 169–88, Ives sets out a model of Henrician Court politics in which policies and key decisions are driven by Henry VIII's advisers and their clienteles, who jockey for power and influence. Now generally considered to be too schematic, this approach followed a trail blazed in the mid twentieth century by G. R. Elton, for almost forty years the pre-eminent Tudor specialist.

According to Elton, Henry VIII was little more than a lazy, greedy opportunist, who needed his ministers to tell him how to make a better world. Elton's famous trilogy on Thomas Cromwell, comprising *The Tudor Revolution in Government, Policy and Police: The Enforcement of the Reformation in the Age of Thomas Cromwell* and *Reform and Renewal: Thomas Cromwell and the Common Weal* (Cambridge: Cambridge University Press, 1953–73), set the benchmark for the serious study of Tudor primary sources, but few experts now concur with his provocative interpretations. Lucidly summed up in his 'Thomas More and Thomas Cromwell', in idem, *Studies in Tudor and Stuart Politics and Government*, 4 vols. (Cambridge: Cambridge University Press, 1974–92), IV, pp. 144–60, Elton's views have recently acquired a new and unexpected resurrection in the novels of Hilary Mantel.

A seminal collection of essays, *The English Court: From the Wars of the Roses to the Civil War*, ed. D. R. Starkey (London: Longman, 1987), is a good starting point for investigating recent, revisionist approaches to the history of the early Tudor Court and royal administration. More credible and sympathetic readings of Cardinal Wolsey than Elton's can be found in the fine scholarly contributions to *Cardinal Wolsey: Church, State and Art*, ed. S. J. Gunn and P. G. Lindley (Cambridge: Cambridge University Press, 1991). Other important guides to these broader themes and issues, including Cromwell, Parliament, the judiciary and the role of the nobility and gentry in politics, can be found in S. J. Gunn's *Early Tudor Government, 1485–1558* (Basingstoke: Macmillan, 1995) and notably in a key collection of reprinted essays by leading experts embracing the wider Tudor period, *The Tudor Monarchy*, ed. J. Guy (London: Arnold, 1997).

Of the towering works of early Reformation history framing Henry VIII's reign, D. MacCulloch's scintillating *Thomas Cranmer: A Life* (New Haven, Conn., and London: Yale University Press, 1996) takes pride of place, closely followed (if from a radically different perspective) by E. Duffy's *The Stripping of the Altars: Traditional Religion in England c.1400–c.1580* (New Haven, Conn., and London: Yale University Press, 1992). On the interface between Court politics and the break with Rome and the dissolution of the monasteries, G. W. Bernard's *The King's Reformation: Henry VIII and the Remaking of the English Church* (New Haven, Conn., and London: Yale University Press, 2005) is the best and most comprehensive study. The author's view of Henry's religion should, however, be read in the light of a transformative scholarly article: R. Rex, 'The Religion of Henry VIII', *Historical Journal*, 57 (2014), pp. 1–32, which establishes definitively that the king was not the 'Erasmian' enthusiast claimed by Bernard.

Lastly, the material culture of Henry VIII and his courtly circle is admirably surveyed in D. R. Starkey's *Henry VIII: A European Court in England* (London: Collins and Brown, 1991), S. Thurley's *The Royal Palaces of Tudor England* (New Haven, Conn., and London: Yale University Press, 1993) and M. Hayward's *Dress at the Court of King Henry VIII* (Leeds: Maney, 2007). Hayward's study is not limited purely to items of clothing, but incorporates a wealth of information on courtly rituals and ceremonies, tastes, fashions and material possessions. The most impressive specific study of early Tudor royal spectacle is T. P. Campbell's *Henry VIII and the Art of Majesty: Tapestries at the Tudor Court* (New Haven, Conn., and London: Yale University Press, 2007), closely followed for portrait painting by S. Foister's *Holbein and England* (New Haven, Conn., and London: Yale University Press, 2004).

Picture Credits

1. Frontispiece of Henry VIII's *Assertio Septem Sacramentorum* (© Biblioteca Apostolica Vaticana)
2. Bust said to be of a young Henry VIII by Guido Mazzoni (Royal Collection Trust, © Her Majesty Queen Elizabeth II, 2014/ Bridgeman Images)
3. The Great Tournament Roll of Westminster showing Henry VIII jousting before Katherine of Aragon (College of Arms, reproduced by permission of the Kings, Heralds and Pursuivants of Arms)
4. The Field of Cloth of Gold (Royal Collection Trust, © Her Majesty Queen Elizabeth II, 2014/Bridgeman Images)
5. Detail of 1527 treaty, E 30/1114 (© National Archives)
6. Henry VIII by Hans Holbein the Younger (Thyssen-Bornemisza Collection, Madrid, Spain/Bridgeman Images)
7. Thomas Cromwell by Hans Holbein the Younger (© Frick Collection)
8. Detail of engraving of the disembowelling of the Carthusian priors (© The Trustees of The British Museum)
9. Detail from Henry VIII's psalter (© The Trustees of the British Library)
10. Engraving of Henry VIII in old age by Cornelis Metsys (Private collection)

Index